The Naked Shepherd

The Naked Shepherd

A PASTOR SHARES
HIS PRIVATE FEELINGS
ABOUT LIVING, WORKING,
AND GROWING TOGETHER
IN THE CHURCH

G. Curtis Jones

WORD BOOKS
PUBLISHER

Library of Congress Catalog Card Number: 79–63935

ISBN 0–8499–2870–2

Printed in the United States of America

To our

Paul and Merry

Both of Whom
Are Ministers

1875 Job Standards for Ecclesiastics

"WANTED—A rector for St. James' Church, Milwaukee, Wisconsin. He must possess all Christian graces and a few worldly ones; must have such tact and disposition as will enable him to side with all parties in the parish on all points, giving offense to none; should possess a will of his own, but agree with all the vestry; must be socially inclined and of dignified manners—affable to all, neither running after the wealthy nor turning his back upon the poor; a man of high-low church tendencies preferred.

"Must be willing to preach first-class sermons and do first-class work at second-class compensation—salary should not be so much of an object as the desire to be a zealous laborer in the vineyard; should be able to convince all that they are miserable sinners without giving offense.

"Each sermon must be short, but complete in itself—full of old-fashioned theology in modern dress—deep, but polished, and free from the eloquence peculiar to newly graduated theologians; should be young enough to be enthusiastic, but possess judgment of one of ripe years and experience.

"He only who possess the above qualifications need apply. To such a one will be given steady employment for a term of years."

From old *Milwaukee Sentinel*, June 16, 1875

Contents

Foreword by Don Carter, Vice President, Knight-Ridder Newspapers, Inc.
Acknowledgments
Preface

1. *His Trials and Temptations*   17

Surviving the Blow/God Telephoned/Vulnerability/Willing Women/No Clock to Punch/Center Stage/Dipping in the Till/Possessive Preachers/A Profile of Christ

2. *His Spiritual Ancestors*   31

Those Who Heard/A Mixed Company/Emerging Ministry/Emerging Church/Visible Link

3. *His Call*   43

The Persistent Call/Parish Pastor/Careers, Occupations, Vocations/As Applied to the Church/Nature of the Call/Equipment and Endowment/Finding the Place/Continuing Development/Women and Ministry/Seminaries Say/Selecting Your Minister/Your Call

4. *His Sermons*   60

What Is a Sermon?/Sermons Change Lives/What Is Preaching?/Labor of Love/Help Your Minister Preach/Are You Expecting Too Much?/Help Him Ring the Bell/Between Two Worlds

5. *His Emotional Load*   75

Unlimited Exposure/Coping with Psyche/Help
Save Your Preacher/Sensitive Souls and Suicide/
Self Portrait/Keeping Well/On Constant Call/Day-
tight Compartments

6. *His Family*   90

Has the Family a Future?/The Preacher's Home/
The Minister's Wife/Love the Children/Options in
Housing/Profile of a Preacher/Higher Compensa-
tion

7. *His Responsibilities*   109

Educator, Physician, Social Worker/Administra-
tor/Ornament/Counselor and Pastor/Evangelist/
Preacher

8. *His Frustrations*   123

Identity Crisis/Titles Seldom Tell/Double Stan-
dards/Inflexibility/Politics of Power/Inertia

9. *His Support*   136

Encouragement/Attitude/Attendance/Joyous Par-
ticipation/Meaningful Gifts/Entertainment/Rec-
reation/Be a Volunteer/Read, Renew, Relate/
Prayer

10. *His Love*   156

Maturing Love/The Language of Love/Profiles of
Love/Echoes of Love/The Life of Love/The Presence of Love

Foreword

I've known and admired the work of Dr. Curtis Jones for a number of years, but rarely have I had such a feast of good reading as I found in the pages of this new volume. Some years ago when I was the executive editor of the *Macon Telegraph and News* and he was a minister in that Georgia city, Dr. Jones wrote a weekly column for our newspapers. Occasionally on his visits to our office, we'd talk about light pleasantries. But I was not a member of his church, and I never had the opportunity to plumb the thoughts and experiences of this gifted man.

Now, in *The Naked Shepherd,* I have this opportunity. In it Dr. Jones strips away some of the curtains we've strung around our pastors and tells us of their trials, their temptations, their responsibilities, their frustrations, their emotional loads, and their commitments.

The book answers questions about ministers that I have often pondered and never quite had the brashness or the opportunity to ask.

About the nature of sermons, for instance: "Do you want your preacher to be such a connoisseur and peddler of words that you are so mesmerized by his cleverness and beautiful ambiguity that you leave corporate worship unconvinced, unchanged, and unchallenged? Is not a Christian sermon supposed to comfort the distressed and disturb the comfortable and complacent?"

In another chapter he explains, "Preaching is strenuous. No one can possibly ring the miracle bell for God every time he stands up to preach. Yet I find a nervous impatience among many congregations with their minister if he does not 'deliver' Sunday after Sunday according to preconceived ideas of preaching."

Dr. Jones minces no words. He says that "nowhere is male chauvinism more pronounced than in the structure and leadership of the modern church" and deplores it.

The book is laced with anecdotes and quotations—some from his own ministry, many from other stalwarts who have spent their lives in the pulpit. Dr. Jones tells us that the "temptations of secular culture" have not passed over the parsonage. "Even though the vast majority of ministers' marriages are stable, divorce is not uncommon among the clergy. Some ministers have drinking problems; some are lazy; some are power-poachers; others have poor credit or poor health. Still others are handicapped by unpredictable wives or problem children."

There are many ways we laymen can help. This fine book suggests several: find things we like in our pastor's sermons and comment favorably on them; provide him a pleasant study to prepare his sermons and do his church work; free him from financial worries with an adequate salary and retirement plan; relieve him of petty distractions so he can proceed with the major obligations of his ministry; bring a spirit of joy and thanksgiving to the church and participate cheerfully in its various programs.

"Your pastor is not perfect," Dr. Jones tells us in one of the eloquent passages of *The Naked Shepherd.* "However, at the core of his being is love. To see him is to feel better; to talk with him is to be encouraged; to pray with him is to find the will to begin again."

I was counseled and inspired as I read this book. I believe laymen will find in it new keys to understanding their pastors and the relationships that bind us together in the service of God. I know I have.

—Don Carter
Group Vice President
Knight-Ridder Newspapers, Inc.

Acknowledgments

As with most undertakings, the production of a book owes much to many contributors. Although I have benefited from research, correspondence, and reliving experiences, I am nevertheless mindful of and grateful for the input of many friends. My debt to persons and publishers is herewith acknowledged and delineated.

Words are inadequate to express appreciation for my readers: Dr. Marvin G. OsbornHolmes Beach, Florida; and Dr. Howard E. Short, St. Louis, Missouri, for their perception and counsel. These professional journalists have assisted me in several projects but never more creatively than in this volume. Moreover, I cite the support of my family, especially my wife Sybil, astute critic, whose companionship and encouragement cannot be confined to a single rubric. I am also grateful to Mildred Patrick for a helpful reading of the material and to my secretary, Nancy Polisky, who labored skilfully on the manuscript.

I recognize the cooperation and generosity of publishers for use of copyrighted materials. Reference to Sir Winston Churchill's conversation with Beverley Nichols in Chapter 1 is from *A Spiritual Autobiography* by William Barclay, Wm. B. Eerdmans Publishing Company, Grand Rapids, Michigan, 1975, p. 23. Used by permission.

Dr. David H. C. Read's definition of preaching, quoted in Chapter 4, is from his book, *Sent from God*, Abingdon Press, Nashville, Tennessee, 1974, p. 14. Used by permission.

In Chapter 6, the quotation from J. Paul Getty is from his autobiography, *As I See It*, published by Prentice-Hall, Inc., Englewood Cliffs, New Jersey, 1976, p. 88. Used by permission.

In Chapter 8, comment directed to the Reverend John C. Harper is taken from his work, *Sunday, A Minister's Story*, published by Little, Brown and Company, Boston, Massachusetts, 1974, p. 40. Used by permission.

A few paragraphs in this same chapter originally appeared in *The Pulpit*, predecessor to *The Christian Ministry*, under the title "Muddle in the Ministry," February, 1968, published by the Christian Century Foundation, Chicago, Illinois. Used by permission. Also in this context are a few sentences from an article in *The Disciple*, April, 1975, "Don't Move the Candles!", published by the Christian Board of Publication, St. Louis, Missouri. Used by permission.

Mention of the "leather sermon case" in Chapter 9 is from William Barclay's *A Spiritual Autobiography*, Wm. B. Eerdmans Publishing Company, Grand Rapids, Michigan, 1975, p. 6. Used by permission.

All Scripture quotations, unless otherwise noted, are from the Revised Standard Version of the Bible, copyrighted 1946, 1952 ©, 1971, 1973 by the Division of Christian Education of the National Council of the Churches of Christ in the United States of America. Used by permission.

Finally, I express deep gratitude to my friends at Word, especially Floyd W. Thatcher, Vice President and Executive Editor, and Al Bryant, Senior Editor, for their advice, time, and total supportiveness.

Preface

An influential layman said of his former minister, "Burt's trouble was he could not make up his mind between being a professional golfer or a preacher."

What is your view of the person who stands up to preach, who visits the sick, buries the dead, confirms declarations of love, and who administers the affairs of the congregation?

Who is this suave "executive" dubbed minister charged with the congregation's gross national product?

Who is this "mousy occupant of the manse" whose long face, thin neck, and clericals silhouette him servant of God's church, or who is his more aggressive counterpart clad in jeans, boots, leather jacket, with flowing mane and crash helmet, poised on a motorcycle?

I know ministers are male and female. However, to avoid repetition of "he/she" phrases throughout the text, I am using the pronoun "he" in the traditional generic sense, meaning the minister, male or female. I am also using the terms "minister," "pastor," and "preacher" interchangeably, realizing that the word "minister" is more comprehensive and includes the work of both pastor and preacher. Names of persons referred to in illustrations are fictitious; the experiences are authentic.

Whatever the sex, circumstance, locale, or denomination, there are some who see the preacher as a kind of spiritual prostitute, exchanging concern and compassion for cash.

Others view this mysterious person not only as a parasite, but also as a terribly presumptuous individual having the audacity to proclaim truth, to declare the acceptable year of the Lord, insisting life has direction and purpose.

Still others turn to the pastor as if he were running an ecclesiastical cafeteria, periodically partaking of what they need without price and frequently without gratitude.

One layman sees the pastor as "that devoted, dedicated Christian who bridges the gap in his generation so that the past and the future are connected."

Still another knowledgable, sensitive Christian wrote: "The preacher is to lead the flock in seeking the truth; truth about God's love and forgiveness, yes. But also the truth about ourselves and our social problems."

The late Karl Barth envisioned the preacher holding up the Bible in one hand and the morning newspaper in the other! Thus, the perceptive soul is able to bring ancient truths to bear upon contemporary issues.

Once the paragon of integrity and affection, like many public servants today the minister has inherited difficult problems, some of his own making, others emanating from spinoffs in a complex, sensual, apathetic society.

George Bernard Shaw maintained that the preacher "must either share the world's guilt or go to another planet." Since few are likely to enjoy such expeditions, he must learn to cope with current pressures and assist others in the art of handling life's tensions and expectations.

The minister must be more than a trained professional, more than a kept person, and more than the keeper of an institution. Unlike other professionals, he is judged by how well his life coincides with the gospel he proclaims. He must take his own medicine, or the prescription is spurious.

If he is to possess a sane, clear, contagious view of community, government, business, and politics, the pastor must seek to understand their nomenclature, systems of operation, and tricks of deception, while being servant of none! St. Francis de Sales said it succinctly: "The knowledge of the priest is the eighth sacrament of the Church."

This book focuses on the parish minister, his heritage, humanity, and mission in our complex, sophisticated society. This person—called by God—does not want to be lionized or placed on a pedestal which inevitably develops disillusionment, divisions, and double standards of behavior. He desires only understanding and support which should accompany Christian commitment and adventure.

The Naked Shepherd endeavors not only to project a clearer and more realistic profile of the minister for lay examination and evaluation of their *mutual relationship,* but also to give pastors an overview of situations, an opportunity to see themselves as others *see them in routine and extraordinary ministries.* It is hoped that an open presentation of lay and clergy roles may be mutually helpful.

Ordination does not set one above his parishioners or fellow travelers, only apart, that he may see more clearly and be seen in the light of the One who said, "I am the way, and the truth, and the life; no one comes to the Father, but by me" (John 14:6).

This book is written in the context of forty years in the ministry, which has included metropolitan pulpits, teaching homiletics in seminary, publishing, lecturing and preaching around the world, and ten years in television and radio programming. From the perspective of experience, and input of many colleagues and friends, the author attempts to dispel myths concerning the ministry; expose the preacher's warts and wings, his eccentricities, frustrations, and fulfillment. This is why we have chosen the title, *The Naked Shepherd.*

By exploring ten common areas of assessment and complaint, the writer seeks to enlarge the reader's view of the minister in general and his pastor in particular. Moreover, it is hoped that the preacher will see himself in *the common mirror of ministry.*

1
His Trials and Temptations

"I know proper committees at the church have recommended you be called as senior minister, but I—and others—intend to see to it that you don't accept. . . ."

He broke my heart, this professional man in the white coat, highly successful by society's standards. A prominent elder in the church I served, he had called me to his office.

At the time, I was an associate of one of America's great preachers, a popular and erudite pulpiteer.

Shortly after I arrived at this metropolitan church, the senior pastor's health began to deteriorate. Gradually, he delegated more and more responsibility; in fact, my workload included being minister of education, basketball coach, membership developer, and stewardship organizer and implementer. In addition, I chauffeured the senior minister!

Much sooner than many had expected, the beloved man resigned, resignation effective one year hence. The situation invited chaos. My responsibilities increased, including preaching.

An effort was made to ascertain the congregation's desires with respect to a new pastor. A search committee was appointed. The retiring minister asked me if I would like to succeed him. In substance, I replied that, while it would be a great honor, I was not sure I was ready for such an arduous ministry.

Meanwhile, members of the congregation and the pulpit committee talked with me regarding the possibility of becoming senior pastor. Eventually and unwisely I consented to be considered. Ultimately, the pulpit committee and the Department of Worship recommended the associate be extended a call to succeed their revered minister.

Meanwhile, there was much behind-the-scene politicking and destructive conversation.

It was in this context that the popular churchman invited me to his office. I had no idea what he wanted. He was suave, professional, and cruel. As he came quickly to the point, the essence of his comment was, ". . . despite official votes in the church, we don't think you are the man for the job. You are too young and inexperienced to follow a prominent preacher." He added a few other barbs to assure me that I would not have the support of the moneyed members.

I listened and left as gracefully as possible.

SURVIVING THE BLOW

Out on the street, I walked in a daze, his words reverberating in my ears. A product of the great depression, reared on a Virginia farm where my father lost all material possessions except real estate, I was accustomed to disappointment and hard work, but not hard words.

As I stumbled toward the parking lot, I wondered about the credibility of the church. What had I done to deserve such a debilitating encounter? It was not because I was lazy or unmindful of my role. It was not because I did not have good academic credentials. It was not because I was lacking in courage; I had gone to Yale with $5.00 in my pocket. The renunciation had come because the "inner circle" of the congregation disapproved.

I drove home, all ten miles through heavy traffic, to unburden my heart to my understanding wife. We had always said we would never stay where we were not wanted, nor would we ever create or support a schism in the church.

After tearful meditation, we decided that, even though we had three small boys and no financial support of any consequence, we would resign the following Sunday.

This took courage! What would we do? We reviewed an earlier proposition from a businessman who had offered me twice my annual salary at the church to join his firm. Although it was a real temptation in the light of possible unemployment at the end of ninety days, we dismissed it. We had prepared for the pastoral ministry and resolved to continue, God willing.

I shall never forget the facial expressions of the worshipers that Sunday when I read my resignation. Those who knew what had transpired were in tears; others looked aghast. Still others did not have the courage nor grace to speak to me after service.

It was a sad morning for the Joneses and for

the church. Driving home, I was physically and
emotionally exhausted. Although we tried to
spare the boys our hurt, they knew something
was wrong and quietly shared in the ritual of
dinner, not the usual happy time about the table.

The counsel of Robert Frost was pertinent and
comforting: "And remember, nothing is momentous. We always think it is, but—nothing
is momentous."

GOD TELEPHONED

Much like the glory of Easter absorbing the
darkness and sadness of Good Friday, God gave
us a miracle about midafternoon. The telephone
rang. It was long distance. The chairman of the
pulpit committee of an historic congregation
called to invite me to become its pastor.

Being a perceptive attorney and knowing that
the propriety of such an approach was highly
irregular if not unprecedented, he took several
minutes to explain why they were extending a
call in such a manner and the situation at their
church. He assured me they had followed my
ministry, had heard me preach at least once,
and were unanimous in believing I was the person to assist them in relocating their congregation, a decision they had already made, property
acquired. At the end of that long telephone conversation, I accepted the invitation. It was subsequently confirmed in writing. We went and
never had a happier nor more productive pastorate. The Lord continues to work in mysterious ways his ministries to perform.

Not as dramatically, perhaps, as the experience here cited, but every minister has encoun-

tered to some degree utter disillusionment and disappointment with the functioning of the church, or, should I say, its officials. Such conflicts have contributed to an alarming exodus from the ministry; others have reduced pastors to bloodless warriors; still others to lifeless robots waiting for retirement.

Emerging from such experiences, many pastors have been able to identify with George Tyrell of England who, expelled from the Jesuit Order, declared that he was frequently tempted to give up the struggle, "but always the figure of that strange man hanging on the cross sends me back to my tasks again."

And so it does!

VULNERABILITY

There is precious little physical or financial security in the ministry. Tenure is tenuous. Any sermon any Sunday may precipitate dismissal.

The preacher is not a heavenly fallout, but a sensitive human being susceptible to all the frailties and temptations of competitors in this arena called life. The malleability of the minister cannot be appreciated apart from his desire to discover and maintain a meaningful identity in the workaday world and with his guiding relations: God, Christ, and the church.

Sooner or later the conscientious minister (especially young ones bubbling with ambition and blessed with an assortment of gifts) is tempted to turn in his ordination papers, exchanging them for contractual agreements collectible under the law. The temptation to quit is nowhere more prevalent than among those called to preach. However, this is by no means the minister's only temptation. Consider for a moment one seldom mentioned until a pastor runs away with the organist: namely, sexual attraction to female counselees and parishioners.

If one's exposure in this area needs documentation, or if one needs to be alerted to the adroit dangers of certain types of women in the church, read Dr. Charles L. Rassieur's book, *The Problem Clergy Don't Talk About.* As Executive Director of the Institute of Pastoral Care, Harrisburg, Pennsylvania, he shares anonymously a wide spectrum of sexual attractions and how respective pastors have coped. Dr. Rassieur concludes, "More apparent than anything else is the need for parish pastors to integrate their intellectual theology with their visceral humanity."

WILLING WOMEN

Martha, an attractive, well-to-do widow who loves the church, attends regularly and pops in and out of the pastor's office frequently to say "hello." She also selects odd hours when the children are in school or away to invite the pastor over for tea. When he arrives, the atmosphere is conducive for lovemaking. Martha is seductively dressed. How does the minister cope with such temptation without succumbing?

Virginia is not a member of the parish. She is well-schooled and traveled; she is attracted to the pastor, partly because of his personality and mind, and partly because of his body. An involvement with him would help to justify her own guilt. She comes to his study too often, each time staying much too long.

Take the case of Sarah, whose first marriage was a catastrophe. She is far from well. One day she called asking the pastor to drop by her home between four and five o'clock in the afternoon. When Brother Johnson rang the doorbell, a voice called out, "Come in. Is that you, Mr. Johnson?"

"Yes it is," he replied.

"Would you mind coming back to my bedroom? I am not feeling very well today."

Innocently enough, he went, only to find a very beautiful woman, exquisitely gowned, lying on the bed with a sheet carelessly draped over her.

There are a number of situational factors which stimulate sexual interest. It sometimes occurs in the discussion of sexual material. Perhaps the woman is describing her inadequate relations with her husband or someone else. Again, from subtle clues—language, dress, life style—the pastor may conclude the woman before him is sexually available. Another factor arousing the counselor's sexual stimulation may be triggered by the observation that the desperate counselee is dependent upon him or that he meets some of her criteria for love.

The minister is constantly exposed to sex exploitation. A pastor's happy marriage and satisfactory sex relations will not in themselves prevent sexual attraction to other women, but they will assist him in dealing with the temptation, enabling him to be more aware of cunning, willing women and the necessity to develop preventive disciplines.

The preacher has a variety of ways to prevent such advances: such as telling the secretary— or reiterate to himself—that when Martha comes the door must be left open or he must establish a time limit for visits.

Another physical deterrent is to sit behind one's desk with the counselee directly before him. Maintaining a professional stance is important. Still another caution is to refrain from any type of intimacy or familiarity, such as the use of first names or touching the other person.

Like all perceptive persons, the minister knows what setting or overtures "turn him on" sexually, and he should strive to prevent their occurrence.

Strangely enough, lay people, who are otherwise generous and forgiving when the pastor is derelict in discipline, are slow to forgive the slightest sexual impropriety. As prominent United States Senators have discovered, it requires more than quoting Jesus' conversation with the ancient scribes and Pharisees near the temple, regarding the woman taken in adultery and his admonition, "Let him who is without sin among you be the first to throw a stone at her" (John 8:7), to quiet the critics! It requires stern self-discipline, which comes with constant renewal of Christian purpose. No one knows better than the minister that life is self-determining.

NO CLOCK TO PUNCH

Unlike other professional persons, the pastor has considerable freedom in determining working hours. His work is not laid out for him; he receives no sound or command to begin his day, save those that are self-imposed. Since there is so much freedom at the pastor's disposal, it requires great discipline to determine and maintain a respectable and productive schedule.

There is little place in the Lord's work for a lazy person. In discussing a colleague, a friend commented, "Jim is a nighter. . . . Then no one can find him during morning hours." Anyone entering the ministry will soon discover that God's work cannot be accomplished in an eight-hour day or a forty-hour week. Moreover, the business and industrial communities have little respect for a minister who is irregular in office hours, puts in a short day, is forever taking coffee breaks and roaming the streets, not to help people, but to avoid those committed to his charge!

Once after returning from a speaking engagement out of the city, I asked the senior custodian about the Sunday service and the associate's sermon. Unhesitatingly he replied, "He put the time in!" One who proclaims and strives to practice the Good News must put in more time than his adversaries. Screwtape's captives are always attempting to discourage early rising, launching of a worthy project, making calls in the afternoon, and having the sermon ready by Friday. The preacher must guard against what Goethe called "morning slackness."

I have been so conscious of this complaint and possibility in my own life that, through the years, I have slept with two clocks by my bed, one electric, one manual. Regardless of schedule and night meetings, the alarm went off daily at 6:15 A.M.

If one permits himself to drift with his feelings, it not only precludes personal growth, but it also delays the coming of the kingdom. The community soon learns if the minister is truly about his Father's business. One is reminded of the conversation between Beverley Nichols and Winston Churchill. Mr. Nichols had just published *Prelude,* an instant success. When Mr. Churchill asked about his writing disciplines, Nichols replied he waited for the mood, the inspiration. Churchill retorted, "Nonsense. You should go to your room every morning at nine o'clock, and say, 'I am going to write for four hours.' "

The startled Mr. Nichols asked what would happen if he should have "toothache, indigestion, or the inability to get down to it"?

Sir Winston rejoined, "You've got to get over that. If you sit waiting for inspiration, you will sit waiting until you are an old man. . . . Kick yourself; irritate yourself; but write; it's the only way."

CENTER STAGE

Beyond biological allurements and physical slackness are the egocentric temptations; the temptation to succeed, to make it big, to have the largest and richest church in the denomination.

Jesus faced temptation. However interpreted, the wilderness experiences provided the Lord opportunity to reassess himself, his mission, and his approach to ministry. The devil tested him at vulnerable points, especially in the second temptation, where the emphasis was on acceptance and success. "And the devil took him up, and showed him all the kingdoms of the world in a moment of time, and said to him, 'To you I will give all this authority and their glory; for it has been delivered to me, and I give it to whom I will. If you, then, will worship me, it shall all be yours' " (Luke 4:5–7).

"Jesus answered him, 'It is written, 'You shall worship the Lord your God, and him only shall you serve' " (Luke 4:8).

Here Jesus was tempted to make it to the top, to yield to secular definitions of success. It was a pitch for self-advancement, security, popularity.

The temptation to be popular forever plagues the pastor. It expresses itself in many forms, but nowhere more graphically than when he is preparing the sermon. "Shall I feed the sheep Sunday or amuse the goats? Shall I seek to interpret the gospel as it relates to Main Street, or shall I pick up a few serendipities from the sports page?"

This thirst for popularity, frequently accompanied by vanity, pride, artificiality, and arrogance, reduces the preacher to a showman, the sermon to a Sunday sedative.

The egocentric minister who is unable or unwilling to delegate responsibility, who must always have his way, is not only in danger of separating himself from his people, but also from his Lord.

DIPPING IN THE TILL

Likewise, preachers are tempted to be careless in financial matters. Roger was a fine man, well-trained and gifted. However, he permitted himself to become too involved in the finances of the church, handled a great deal of money, reported to no one, and was a poor administrator

of the budget. Eventually, like Judas, he began
to borrow from the treasury. He did not intend
to steal, simply to borrow enough to tide him
over to the next payday. The lack of financial
credibility left his ministry in shambles.

Practically every congregation has at least one
person who is far more competent in money
matters than the preacher; laity should be alert
to this truth and protect their pastor.

POSSESSIVE PREACHERS

Preachers also have a tendency to become
possessive, expecially as they grow older. Uncon-
sciously they use such phrases as "my church,"
"my pulpit," "my people." One of the real dangers, I think, in a long pastorate, is that the
preacher not only is accepted as a fixture in command of the entire operation, but his creativity
is minimized because of relatively few changes.
To many, he *is* the church. Whatever Brother
Brown says is gospel. He speaks *ex-cathedra*.
Such a shepherd must persistently avoid the
temptation of becoming the pet lamb of the congregation!

Despite residual imperfections of the minister, the majority of pastors are challenged to
be like Jesus, to give him first place in their lives,
to program their preaching, to be "slaves of Jesus
Christ," to be willing to be led by his Spirit,
and to serve wherever needed with courage and
compassion.

Christians are seeking a victory that over-
comes worldly ways and wickedness. It is the
victory of patience over impatience, gentleness
over harshness, trust over fear, faith over doubt,
and love over hate.

A PROFILE OF CHRIST

Above the vicissitudes and temptations of the parish minister stands the tested and triumphant memory of Jonathan Edwards. He was born in East Windsor, Connecticut, October 5, 1703. His father was minister of the Congregational village church for sixty-four years. Jonathan entered Yale at thirteen, graduating at seventeen. Following seminary and ordination, he associated himself with his grandfather, Solomon Stoddard, who preached in Northhampton, Massachusetts. At the age of twenty-six, when the old man died, Jonathan became minister of this large church.

Five years later he stepped into pulpit fame, being one of the most original theologians in America and a pioneering evangelist in New England. Eventually, revival enthusiasm waned; controversy developed. Not a single person united with the church for four years. Agitation for a new minister spread. Bitterness grew. Finally, in 1750, the church dismissed its distinguished pastor. Jonathan Edwards was then forty-seven years old with a wife and ten children to support.

Time passed. Soon the Northhampton church discovered their former minister was not easily replaced. Chagrined officials asked Dr. Edwards to supply until a pastor could be secured. Imagine one returning with grace to the pulpit from which he had been fired! He supplied until his successor was called.

Then the only church open to him was a small congregation in Stockbridge, Massachusetts, where he served as missionary to the Housatonic Indians.

In spite of harsh treatment and hardships, he maintained a beautiful spirit. It was in this obscure parish that he wrote some of his finest works, including *Freedom of the Will.* From this unsung pulpit, in 1757, Jonathan Edwards was called to the presidency of the College of New Jersey, now Princeton.

Acknowledging frailties and unfaithfulness, the minister knows the gift is still in "earthen vessels," and confidently asserts, "I decided to know nothing among you except Jesus Christ and him crucified. And I was with you in weakness and in much fear and trembling; and my speech and my message were not in plausible words of wisdom, but in demonstration of the Spirit and power, that your faith might not rest in the wisdom of men but in the power of God" (1 Cor. 2:2–5).

2

His Spiritual

Ancestors

Who is this soul so strongly tempted? Who is this mysterious messenger? Who is this friendly stranger who reminds us of God and has the audacity to speak for him?

God has commissioned men and women in all generations to be his ambassadors.

Consider Abraham and Sarah who heard Yahweh's message. Sarah, much too old to conceive, nevertheless bore Isaac when Abraham was one hundred years old and she was ninety! Following decisive events, the Lord said to Abraham: "Take your son, your only son Isaac, whom you love, and go to the land of Moriah, and offer him there as a burnt offering upon one of the mountains of which I shall tell you" (Gen. 22:2).

What a directive! One wonders how Abraham endured the command and prepared for the journey. Imagine his trauma and agony—the boy's questions. As they neared the place of sacrifice, Isaac exclaimed: "Behold, the fire and the wood; but where is the lamb for a burnt offering?" (Gen. 22:7ff). His father answered: "God will provide himself the lamb for a burnt offering, my son."

Abraham built an altar, bound Isaac, and laid him on it. As the sorrowful father lifted the knife to slay his son, the Lord said: "Do not lay your hand on the lad or do anything to him; for now I know that you fear God, seeing you have not withheld your son, your only son, from me" (Gen. 22:12).

Because of his obedience, God blessed and prospered Abraham saying: "And your descendants shall possess the gate of their enemies, and by your descendants shall all the nations of the earth bless themselves, because you have obeyed my voice" (Gen. 22:17b–18).

At least twelve centuries before Christ the old patriarch of Mesopotamia demonstrated such courage and truth that he was affectionately honored as the father of his nation.

THOSE WHO HEARD

Moses, who was saved from the cruelty of Pharaoh by the cleverness of his mother and courage of his sister Miriam, later was summoned by God to lead the children of Israel out of Egyptian bondage. At the time of his encounter he was tending sheep near Mt. Horeb. Stunned and inarticulate, he desperately tried to evade the command. "Who am I," he retorted, "that I should go to Pharaoh . . . ?" (Exod. 3:11). Moses procrastinated and suggested his more articulate brother Aaron for the assignment. At last the exasperated shepherd asked, "If I come to the people of Israel and say to them, 'The God of your fathers has sent me to you,' and they ask me, 'What is his name?'

what shall I say to them?" (Exod. 3:13). The Lord answered: "I AM WHO I AM" (3:14).

Ultimately, reluctant and vacillating, Moses became the magnificent Hebrew statesman, lawgiver, and leader who extricated his people from Pharaoh's merciless serfdom.

How could one overlook the dramatic and compelling story of Samuel who, as a boy, ministered under Eli at the temple? "And the word of the Lord was rare in those days; there was no frequent vision" (1 Sam. 3:1).

Eli, old and failing, lay resting. The dull, monotonous days dragged by like weary slaves at sunset. Young Samuel dreamed of God! Whatever the explanation, the lad heard a voice: "Samuel! Samuel!" (3:4).

The astonished boy jumped up and ran to the priest, saying: "Here I am!" (3:5). Eli said he had not called. Like a trumpeter in the morning, a second time the voice awakened Samuel. Again the excited young man hurried to the side of the old judge and priest of Shiloh, who once more assured his associate he had not called. When the restless trainee heard the piercing voice a third time, having been prepared by Eli's counsel, Samuel immediately replied: "Speak, for thy servant hears" (3:10).

In some centering moment, very personal and persuasive, God bids every Christian to rise and bear witness. In the ecstasy of this discovery, dimensions of life are determined or denied.

Such a declaration is supported by the rise and development of leadership in ancient Israel. Although Moses had rescued many from Egypt and had united various tribes, there were different types of people to be served.

There were the pastoral folk, whose wealth

consisted primarily of sheep, cattle, camels, and goats.

A second characteristic of early Semitic peoples was the settled tribe, maintaining its identity and occupying a definite geographical area.

A third type is represented in the uniting, either by choice or by conquest, of several tribes to create a more powerful and organized community.

When we first met the Hebrews they were a nomadic people. As Moses taught, they believed their nation was under the watchful eye of Yahweh who lived in the mountains. The formula of adoption, the principle of covenant, which persisted all through the history of Israel, was a simple yet profound proclamation: "I will take you for my people, and I will be your God" (Exod. 6:7).

In her autobiography, *My Life,* Golda Meir says she always had difficulty in believing the "Jews were God's chosen people." Rather, she likes to believe the "Jews were the first people that chose God."

However interpreted, there existed among the early Hebrews a remarkable faith in Yahweh. He was their guide and deliverer, companion and leader in battle. Thus, these nomadic people carried with them portable symbols, stones, which had been given to them at the mountain. These symbols were kept in a closed box, revered and regarded as sacred, down to the destruction of the Temple in 586 B.C.

Over against the primitive faith and simple life style of the Hebrews, we view the Canaanite civilization. It, too, had come from the same general Semitic stock as the Hebrews. Although largely an agricultural people, they had managed to attain a unity which enhanced their strength and effectiveness.

A MIXED COMPANY

The religion of these settled Semitics naturally developed according to conditions and needs. For instance, the tribal god became the local god, the general term being "Baal," a word meaning "owner" and "husband," "slave" and "wife." Thus, the Baal of any region was master of the people; husband of the land. Every village had its "high place"—usually a hilltop or a lovely spot beneath spreading trees where they celebrated worship, observed special days and festivals.

The priest continued to be the most prominent religious official. Although Baals were much in evidence, their dominance was limited to given territories. They were definitely connected with the rites and produce of the soil—gods of fertility.

God was becoming complex. To some he was all but synonymous with Baal. New rituals and practices emerged. Apparently Israel incorporated the cults of the Canaanites, indeed much of their language, into their culture. The high places and sanctuaries of the Canaanites became favorite sites of Yahweh's worship.

It is important to remember that even when the faith of Israel was most contaminated by the religions of the Baals, Yahweh retained a precious remnant on whom he could depend for witness and work.

In Scripture we encounter a mixed company who endeavored to proclaim the will of Yahweh. Among them were the seers and the prophets.

Despite their weaknesses, they were recognized and generally accepted as those in whom God dwelt and through whom he spoke.

The prophets were by far the most profound. In them believers saw the correlation of religion and morality, righteousness and God.

A definite characteristic of the early prophet, as we understand his role, appeared when he separated himself from his tribe or band to fulfill his summons. After discipline and meditation, he would return to deliver a message out of harmony with common utterances and practices.

Micaiah was among the first of these independent spirits. He solemnly foretold King Ahab of Israel and King Jehoshaphat of Judah the sorry fate that would befall them if they attacked Ramoth-gilead. Compensation for his prophecy? Imprisonment. But his words were true. Ahab was killed in battle.

Amos, herdsman from the hill country of Tekoa, disturbed by moral, social, and political conditions, stressed social righteousness. "Let justice roll down like waters," he cried, "and righteousness like an overflowing stream" (5:24). This rugged shepherd and fiery preacher was among the first to declare the universality of Yahweh.

Hosea's concept of a loving God evolved from his experiences with an unfaithful wife, Gomer, a harlot. Possessed by love, he kept her in his household. He saw a parallel between his predicament and Israel's plight. "When Israel was a child, I loved him, and out of Egypt I called my son. The more I called them, the more they went from me . . ." (Hosea 11:1,2). Although the nation had dissipated itself, the prophet believed God still loved his people.

Another powerful agent and spokesman for God was the aristocrat from Jerusalem, Isaiah, whose sheer force of personality, breadth of wisdom, adroitness of statesmanship, beauty and power of speech, distinguished him as an extraordinary man. Being familiar with the power structures of his day, he was able to communicate the urgency of Israel's condition in penetrating terms. This dynamic prophet declared that God, not man, determines history. Therefore, true peace and lasting prosperity can be achieved only by doing the will of God.

At a time when he had grown discouraged in his ministry, Isaiah experienced a dramatic encounter with Yahweh. It was the year that King Uzziah died! Alone in the temple, in the ecstasy of the moment he found himself in an unprecedented worship experience. In his meditation everything assumed gigantic and glorious proportions. As he reflected on the ancient ceremony, so rich in color, symbolism, and music, suddenly the imagery came alive. He was in the presence of God!

Sensing his unworthiness, the prophet cried out: "Woe is me! For I am lost; for I am a man of unclean lips, and I dwell in the midst of a people of unclean lips; for my eyes have seen the King, the Lord of hosts!" (Isa. 6:5).

During this centering and renewing moment, Isaiah heard a voice asking: "Whom shall I send, and who will go for us?" In deep humility and commitment, he answered: "Here am I! Send me" (6:8).

EMERGING MINISTRY

Because of an awareness of the holy, together with an irresistible desire to share truth, love, and faith, an incalculable number of men and women have accepted the challenge to become spiritual ambassadors. Differing in background, capacity, and approach, they nevertheless share the conviction that light dispels darkness; love conquers hate; faith vanquishes doubt; and a more perfect day has come because Christ lives!

Beyond the mighty company of men and women mentioned in Scripture and history, God chose Mary and Joseph to rear his Son. When ancient Palestine was little more than a flea market, Bethlehem's miracle split time in two, revamped the maps of the world, the philosophies and practices of people.

Even as an infant, a lad in the Temple, a young man growing up in Nazareth, Jesus was slowly but effectively accepting his mission. He came preaching: "The time is fulfilled, and the kingdom of God is at hand; repent, and believe in the gospel" (Mark 1:15).

Convinced of his mission, he requested baptism by his cousin, John, whose announcements of eminence permeated the Jordan Valley country. From a prolonged period of final preparation in the wilderness, Jesus returned to Nazareth. And it was in the synagogue where he declared: "The Spirit of the Lord is upon me, because he has anointed me to preach good news to the poor. He has sent me to proclaim release to the captives and recovering of sight to the blind, to set at liberty those who are oppressed, to proclaim the acceptable year of the Lord" (Luke 4:18,19).

From this prophetic stance, he left the synagogue to implement his commission in a dangerous world. He selected twelve men to share in his ministry—not a celebrity among them! Together they permeated the dark corners of Palestine, uncovering graft and corruption, challenging those in authority, and announcing the kingdom of God. Religious and civic leaders could no longer tolerate their exposure, so they conspired in his crucifixion.

Much to the surprise of Jesus' enemies and the reassurance of his friends, the crucifixion was not final; it was only a brief interruption in his ministry of reconciliation and redemption.

The resurrection placed Bethlehem and Jerusalem in eternal perspective. The cradle and the cross were from the same wood. Those who experienced the ecstasy of Easter could never again be timid, suspicious, or disloyal.

The ministry of Jesus was characterized by his reverence for life, his humanity—the nature and needs of the men and women whom he encountered and served. His understanding of and relationship to God the Father compelled him to look upon all people with compassion.

EMERGING CHURCH

The once rugged, vacillating, hot-tempered Simon Peter was the powerful preacher at Pentecost—the fiftieth day following Easter. He reminded the multitude of their guilt and sin. The people were stunned and frightened by the clarity and power of his words. They exclaimed: "What shall we do?" (Acts 2:37).

"The Big Fisherman" replied: "Repent, and be baptized every one of you in the name of Jesus Christ for the forgiveness of your sins; and you shall receive the gift of the Holy Spirit" (Acts 2:38).

The body of Christ, the church, was being actualized. Many appointees became enthusiastic evangelists, sharing their resources, confirming their faith through good works and worship. The colony of heaven on earth was increasing in numbers and influence.

Some who had vigorously attempted to thwart the early Christian movement now joined in the crusade. Foremost among these was Paul, who, after his encounter on the road to Damascus, exclaimed: "Woe to me if I do not preach the gospel!" (1 Cor. 9:16).

Preaching has seldom been popular. Truth is not easily disseminated and accepted. In every generation, God has had his martyrs, eloquent teachers, powerful preachers, courageous disciples. Faith is never without its witnesses.

"FORWARD THROUGH THE AGES"

On a distant day, from the cross, Jesus said: "Father, forgive them; for they know not what they do" (Luke 23:34). Those words came down to Polycarp, the courageous old bishop of Smyrna, who, before being burned at the stake, responded to the proconsul's urging to revile Christ by exclaiming: "Eighty and six years have I served Him and He hath done me no wrong. How then can I speak evil of my King who saved me?" They came to Martin Luther standing trial at Worms, declaring: "I cannot and will not recant anything, for to go against conscience is neither right nor safe. God help me. Amen." God has had a glorious procession of stalwart souls who would rather die in faithful service than live by false principles.

There has been an unfailing succession of Dietrich Bonhoeffers, Jim Elliots, Paul Carlsons, Peter Marshalls, Albert Schweitzers, and Mother

Teresas. God's servants, his chosen ones, know no boundaries of race, sex, or station. Commitment to Christ is the overarching criterion, love their technique, and faith their companion.

Many have been the changes in priesthood since its identity with Aaron and his descendants. As with other vocations, the outward forms of ministry have changed, but its principal commitment—communicating God's love—has remained constant and contagious. In some instances the ministry has become so professionalized and institutionalized, that individuals feel more like software in a computer than hungry persons reaching out for encouragement and compassion.

VISIBLE LINK

Whether male or female, seminary graduate, proud recipient of a Ph.D., or a licensed itinerant rural preacher, your pastor is numbered among the practitioners of the Great Physician, the compelling Teacher, the perfect Preacher. When appraising him, do not overlook his spiritual ancestors. He is aware of his kinsmen—conscious of their contributions and your expectations.

A pastor is not only minister of the gospel; he is also minister of the church, with an involved organization to direct. He must train and work with volunteers, frequently limited in ability and commitment.

Your minister is not only a student of religious tradition and practice, but he is also a preacher, a family consultant, social psychiatrist, educator, arbitrator, community leader, a friend to the friendless—a person relied upon for guidance, encouragement, contagious good will, and support. His is the most difficult and, at the same time, most rewarding task in the world.

When Queen Elizabeth visited the United States during its Bicentennial celebration, Malcolm Muggeridge's assessment of the British monarchy was frequently quoted: "It provides a bridge between what is functioning and what is everlasting in human affairs."

Ministers of Christ, pastors of the church, are not aristocrats bridging an overrated, selfish past, but presume only to be the unprotected heralds of the Lord sharing the burdens of the oppressed, the ego overloads of the elite, the joys and sorrows of the faithful. Your preacher is the visible link between man's collapsible society and God's indestructible kingdom.

Remember Jesus' words addressed to earlier disciples: "You did not choose me, but I chose you and appointed you that you should go and bear fruit and that your fruit should abide; so that whatever you ask the Father in my name, he may give it to you. This I command you, to love one another" (John 15:16,17).

This is our common heritage and challenge!

3
His Call

The militant agnostic Robert Ingersoll is reported to have said that a typical ministerial candidate would be, "A young man of religious turn of mind and consumptive habit of body, not quite sick enough to die, nor healthy enough to be wicked."

Although the church does not sponsor award nights when members and leaders are hilariously "roasted," nor are Oscars given to the best actors and actresses in the congregation, nor are scholarships established in the names of those exhibiting the largest spiritual muscles on Sunday, Christian disciplines are nonetheless demanding. Ministers must be strong: in body, mind, and heart.

Through the years and with increasing integrity, the church has endeavored to maintain a high level of physical, intellectual, moral, and spiritual wellness for its ministers. This is conceptualized to mean more than good health, rather a dynamic condition wherein the individual is forever attempting to climb higher and

nearer his Christian potential for service. The
well-integrated, committed person is serious
about maximizing his ability, not alone for himself, but for others.

THE PERSISTENT CALL

Following Andrew Young's appointment as
U.S. Ambassador to the United Nations, he was
interviewed by CBS. When asked why he took
the position, which imposes personal and financial burdens over against the easier life style
of a U.S. Congressman, he replied, 'You might
say it was a religious decision."

Every person must find himself in the scheme
of things, and, through careful, critical self-anal-
ysis and counsel, make vocational decisions.
When these are made unselfishly they are, in
reality, religious decisions, which may have extended and far-reaching influence. Who would
deny that Mr. Young's pulpit as Ambassador to
the UN is more powerful than preaching in At-
lanta? His is a world ministry, his pulpit portable.

Paul said, "Now there are varieties of gifts,
but the same Spirit; and there are varieties of
service, but the same Lord; and there are varieties of working, but it is the same God who inspires them all in every one" (1 Cor. 12:4–6).

The Christian is not frustrated by the so-called
dichotomy between secular and sacred work.
Every follower of Christ is called to bear fruit
(John 15:16). God is Lord of all life. Should not
the farmer be as confident of his calling as the
statesman, the mechanic as the minister, the
schoolteacher as the banker? These ministries
may all become holy provided those who prac-

tice their disciplines place human beings before personal gain, accept their work and fulfill it in the context of love. Whatever contributes to human welfare is a sacred vocation; whatever impairs human maturity, irrespective of its prestigiousness, is secular and sinful.

Throughout history there seems to have been considerable emphasis placed on a specific and traceable "call" to preach and teach the gospel. This is not to imply that the druggist, engineer, and athlete are less certain of their commitments, but that, in some centering moment of growing clarity and reality, the preacher has felt, as Peter Marshall put it, "The tap on the shoulder."

This sense of spiritual summoning has resulted in individuals assuming a wide variety of Christian responsibilities ranging from teaching a church school class, preaching, serving in hospitals, to being God's ambassador in distant lands. Paul included all committed workers when he declared, "So, whether you eat or drink, or whatever you do, do all to the glory of God" (1 Cor. 10:31).

The continuing relevance of the Protestant Reformation, its persuasive arguments, remind us that all believers are priests under God, who expect all to communicate the Good News where they work and live. William Carey, first missionary to India, asserted that he preached and taught the gospel "and pegged shoes to pay expenses."

The Christian community has never relegated total responsibility for the ongoing of the kingdom to a clerical caste, to a unique if not strange group of men and women, divinely authorized

to tell others of their freedom in Christ and forgiveness of sins through the miracle of God's
love demonstrated at Calvary. Rather, "the company of the committed" has sought out, encouraged, and assisted in the training of those among
them who, by natural endowments and spirit,
possess the basic qualifications for Christian leadership to assist in the ministry of reconciliation.
Following prescribed studies, disciplines, and
experiences, the church, according to its doctrine and practices, ordains these individuals to
teach and preach the gospel of Christ. These
persons are set apart from—not above—their
peers in a special service of consecration and
commission.

The Bible is replete with examples of individuals, from Isaiah to Paul, who were specifically
challenged to witness for God. He guides his
children through the maze of human confusion
and choice to find and accept a place to communicate Christ's love.

PARISH PASTOR

The pastoral ministry is distinct from general
service rendered to humanity. Many seminaries
are training people to become community or-
ganizers, therapists, counselors, teachers,
church administrators, and a variety of other
excellent vocations. Each one can be a significant Christian ministry, as no one model is su-
perimposed. However, we're considering a
Christian minister as one having heard and responded to the call from God to *preach*, who
believes in the validity and indestructibility of
the church, ordained as a proclaimer of the gos-

pel, responding to a call from a congregation to render an ordered and accountable ministry within the covenants of a Christian community.

The power and presence of the pastor cannot be measured by secular criteria of relevance or respectability—only by his faithfulness to the Word of God, his consistency in articulating the hope that is within him. He does not wait for society to dictate his agenda. Scripture and sensitivity are constantly reminding him of his duties and responses.

Unlike other professionals, your pastor does not have a clientele or patients; he has a community. From both stationary and portable pulpits he speaks to a world under judgment and of a world to come; he voices the warnings and promises of Jesus. He is more than a professional possessing a special expertise; the parish pastor is God's agent of reconciliation, your best friend and supporter.

CAREERS, OCCUPATIONS, VOCATIONS

Definitions may be helpful. A career is usually considered the continuum along which an individual lives out his occupational choice. He may have a number of occupations and jobs within a given sector. Some of these endeavors will be more productive, remunerative, and satisfying than others. However, they still constitute one's career—his life's direction.

An occupation is a field of endeavor, a profession, trade, or skill, by which one earns his living. The majority of us are engaged in some occupation; teaching, practicing law, farming, medicine, music, industry, and the performing arts

are all familiar examples of day-to-day employment. We refer to professions as areas of work
within an occupational sector. We use the word
"role" to delineate responsibilities, functions,
and tasks to be performed by an employee.

A vocation is more inclusive. It is one's total
response to life! Beyond bread-and-butter demands, at best, one's vocation actualizes his mo-
tivating concerns; his willingness to meet life,
to sacrifice for what he believes. One's calling,
one's work should dramatize his values, arrange
priorities, determine disciplines.

As Elton Trueblood and others have suggested, regardless of one's occupational involvement, employment, or means of support, his
central vocation is to bear witness to the presence and love of Jesus Christ. In fact, the most
influential sermons frequently come, not from
ornate pulpits, but from shops, offices, and
homes where individual Christians in daily encounters attract others by the roots of their genuineness.

Career planners would have difficulty placing
Jesus in America's success syndrome but would
be among the first to acknowledge his spiritual
motivation, his all-encompassing ministry to human beings. Referred to as "Teacher," "Rabbi,"
"Physician," "Master," and "Lord," he was recognized, revered, and loved for what he did.

AS APPLIED TO THE CHURCH

In the vocabulary of the church, historically,
the word "vocation" has been restricted to a
specific call from God or the church to give full-
life commitment to Christ. Although terms and

conditions have changed over the years, and although one may be committed to a religious persuasion and life style that does not demand being a full-time resident in the Christian community, it is nonetheless significant.

However, in this instance we're considering the minister—male or female—who, in response to a definite spiritual encounter and intellectual persuasion, is attempting to answer God's call to serve his people by ministering to a given church and community.

As with others, ministers come to their work from varied backgrounds and circumstances. Many can identify with Charles W. Colson who writes of being *Born Again*. Through a dramatic and devastating chain of events, an individual is able, after counsel, prayer, and self-examination, to evaluate his shabby past and experience new life in Christ. There is a resurgence of purpose and will. His life is changed! This is a twice-born person. Such a call to minister is more easily dated and tracked than when one is born into a Christian home, never having known serious conflict nor eroding corruption. Gradually he migrates toward the church and its ministries. A multitude of preachers have come to the pulpit through this exposure. I did. My father, a farmer, an elder in our congregation, challenged me to become a minister. My pastor, mother, and members of the church encouraged me. A black laborer, a lay preacher on our farm, who rose to the office of bishop in his church, practiced his sermons on me. He thrilled my soul!

It would be good to know how and why your pastor made the decision to follow the Galilean

into the pastoral ministry. This is not to suggest
that you debate the sincerity of his call or the
authenticity of his credentials, but rather to better understand the one who stands up to preach.

NATURE OF THE CALL

The late Professor H. Richard Niebuhr helps
clarify the call to serve Christ in his provocative
book, *The Purpose of the Church and Its Ministry.* In it he suggests four definitive calls. To
begin with, one is called to be Christian, which
may variously be described as a call to repen-
tance, faith, baptism, and fellowship in the
church. It is a call to discipleship. Then there
is the secret call when the disciple of Christ experiences an irresistible persuasion or hears the
direct voice of God challenging him to take up
the work of the ministry. The providential call
is an invitation to assume the work of ministry
which comes through the natural equipment of
a person with talents necessary for the exercise
of the responsibilities of the office, relying on
divine guidance for his life's development. Finally, Dr. Niebuhr refers to the ecclesiastical
call, an invitation extended by the Christian
community or the institutional church to engage
in the work of ministry.

The church everywhere and always has expected its servants to have a personal sense of
Christian vocation when committing themselves
to the work of the ongoing kingdom.

However defined or experienced, your pastor's call to the ministry, insofar as humans can
discern, involves his surrender to the will of God
and loyalty to the Lordship of Christ. Hence

he offers himself as a penitent participant in the drama of salvation.

EQUIPMENT AND ENDOWMENT

God's ambassadors should be wholesome, well-rounded, sensitive souls. Whatever their special gifts, acquired graces and cultivated skills, they come from God. Your minister did not create his talents; he and others have nurtured them.

Whatever your pastor's strengths and weaknesses, he does not stand up to preach because he is better than his neighbors and parishioners; he aspires to preach because he has heard the voice of God calling, has experienced conversion, knows purpose for his life in Christ, and is compelled to share.

Contagious, effective servants are usually found in sturdy bodies. There are, of course, many outstanding exceptions to the rule: the apostle Paul, John Calvin, John Knox, William Ellery Channing, Toyohiko Kagawa, and Joni Eareckson to mention a few. He who is dwarfed by nature is inclined to bring a corresponding stature into the leadership of the church.

A minister's gifts must always be evaluated in the context of the church. Apart from sacred history, God's commission, and the Christian community, he has no enduring identity. The pastor is a human being, so allow him to behave like one. Surely there are activities he may engage in which his parishioners may not; some of his members may do things which the minister considers unbecoming a Christian. Even so, the preacher must guard against self-righteous-

ness as if he alone, to quote Paul Scherer in
the 1943 Yale Lecture on Preaching, "had suc-
ceeded in putting a pinch of salt on the tails
of the seven deadly virtues!"

FINDING THE PLACE

It is interesting to observe how and why individuals follow certain careers. Some, of course,
inherit a business; others find their jobs through
and by an amazing chain of circumstances ranging from knowing the right person at the right
time to an unexpected recommendation from
one in power. Some pursue a life's work after
scientific testing and rigorous schooling. Others
work not because of any overpowering conviction of value, aptitude, or training, but simply
as a means of "keeping bread on the table."
Some surveys indicate that approximately one-
half of employed Americans dislike their work.
It is a paying job, not a satisfying vocation.

Still others hear a summons from God to pursue a certain profession or career. I remember
one Saturday evening when I was thinking
through Sunday's responsibilities, trying to absorb the sermon, one of our fourteen-year-old
twins came in and lay on the bed beside me.
In a pensive mood he said, "Dad, when I grow
up, I think I would like to be a medical missionary."

"It is a worthy ambition," I assured him.

We pursued the dream.

To date, he has made two service journeys
to Africa. He is an orthopedic surgeon.

Sometimes this awareness of vocation comes
early. Then again, late. Irrespective of chrono-

logical age, it is usually accompanied by a keen sense of commitment to a life's work; values are rearranged, and a period of preparation assumed.

CONTINUING DEVELOPMENT

Whereas the minister may not be the best-educated person in the community, he is still one of the better-informed individuals. If he has followed recommended educational steps in his schooling, his training will compare favorably with that of other professionals. He will have been exposed to from four to eight years of higher education, depending on his field and practicing interests. In addition, the chances are he will have had clinical experience, a student parish, an internship, or perhaps a year or two as an associate under a seasoned pastor before assuming responsibility for a local congregation.

The judge of a superior court, active in his denomination, wrote me on this point: "I believe in an educated and seminary-trained clergy, and further I believe the educational process does not end with the final degree." The judge continued by saying he esteemed the quality in a minister that allows for continuing development as an open person willing to listen to contemporary ideas "but also to the contemporary urgings of the Holy Spirit."

WOMEN AND MINISTRY

Nowhere is male chauvinism more pronounced than in the structure and leadership of the modern church. Even though the Bible is stippled with the names of such wondrous women as Ruth, Esther, Rahab, Rachel, Lydia, Dorcas, Mary, Martha, and Mary the mother of Jesus, the Christian community has been slow to acknowledge the significant role women have played in the expansion and enrichment of Christianity. In many instances the visible church would be less volatile and effective were it not for the faithfulness of its women.

In increasing numbers women are answering the call to render specific Christian ministries, including the parish. While resistance is softening, it is still rugged and regrettable. The persistence of qualified women to enter the vocations of the church represents more than status-seeking, more than a vendetta against the patriarchal protocol of the church, more than an extension of the ERA; it is a concrete illustration of the phenomenon of Christian compulsion, the indiscriminate call to serve. God's selective service system transcends traditions and sex. Sainthood and leadership in the church have nothing to do with human gender, but everything to do with humanity and genuineness, Christian faith and love.

Women are receiving calls to serve local congregations. While obstruction has centered around the more formal, ecclesiastically-structured churches, especially Episcopalian and Roman Catholic, it is by no means limited to these communions. To those of us who have served in denominations that have long ordained women to the ministry and elected them to all offices within the church, ordination debates seem passé, incredible for Christians. Were it not so serious, it would be hilarious!

Answering the request that emanated from Catholic priests and laity meeting in Detroit, October, 1976, appealing for the ordination of women as priests, early in February, 1977, the Vatican replied that, no matter what position other churches take, the Roman Catholic Church "does not consider herself authorized to admit women to priestly ordination." According to the report (*Time,* February 7, 1977, p. 65), the Vatican placed considerable emphasis on "natural resemblance" to Christ in the priest. The argument ran, with a woman celebrating the Mass, "it would be difficult to see in the minister the image of Christ."

About the same time the media were reminding us of obstacles women were encountering while aspiring to become ministers and priests, an evangelical periodical featured the picture and story of a bright lady seminarian who was entering the ministry of her church with all the rights and responsibilities pertaining thereto. She intends to work with older citizens. This is refreshing!

What is the stance of your church toward an integrated ministry? Do you automatically rule out women candidates for the pulpit? Other than cooking meals, cleaning the church, preparing the sacraments, raising money, visiting the sick, teaching in the church school, reading Scripture and denominational materials, attending worship—what do they do in your church?

There are situations wherein it would be difficult for a woman to function fully as a minister. This is also true of her male counterpart. Some churches are finding a rich experience in having husband and wife serve in a team ministry. De-

spite built-in prejudices, it is a fact that approximately 30 percent of seminary students today
are women. Will your church provide them with
an opportunity to serve the Lord?

SEMINARIES SAY

Ministers in general and students in particular
are currently demonstrating more confidence
in their vocations. In fact, it is said that seminari-
ans are frequently more certain of the claims
of the gospel for them than many of their profes-
sors, who normally live in ivory towers, having
long since retreated from the front lines of battle.

A few years ago, when antiinstitutionalism was
raging, some pastors, especially younger ones,
felt they needed another profession to insure
their worth and the value of their work. This
attitude is changing. An associate dean of a prestigious divinity school wrote, "I think the new
confidence in the ministry today is related to
the more positive assessment of the institutional
church and the willingness of the people to consider investing their lives in the ministry of the
church itself."

Serious theological students, whether in
school or in the parish, are still interested in
social issues, concerned about hunger, ecology,
and political credibility, and are now seeing
their call, says a seminary professor, "in terms
of helping persons develop the spiritual dimensions of existence."

The growing call to serve Christ in today's
world is also reflected in the increased number
of parttime "tent-making ministries" where individuals earn some financial support through

a commercial connection, yet allow time to assist
the church in its ministries to the community.
Many rural congregations would be all but abandoned were it not for the availability of these
dedicated servants.

SELECTING YOUR MINISTER

Assuming proper committees and the congregation have followed your denominational
guidelines in selecting the candidate under consideration as a possible pastor, make sure he is
provided with an overall profile of your church.
This accurate summary of program, detailing
problems, goals, and future projects, should also
include a section on what is expected of the min-
ister.The individual being interrogated has every right to articulate his faith, concept of the
church, and what he would expect in the way
of support should he be called to serve the congregation. When a consensus is reached on relevant issues and concerns, you are ready for the
next step, namely, issuing an invitation or call
to your new minister. Then, install him with
proper ceremony and commitment.

To maximize confidence and to inspire cooperation, to minimize future misunderstandings
and gossip, all agreements should be reduced
to writing and made available to members of
the congregation. This mutually acceptable
statement—or contractual letter—should include all germane assurances such as a free pulpit, tenure, compensation, moving expenses,
housing options, health insurance, pension, staff,
working conditions, automobile expenses, attending conventions and conferences of the
church, acceptance of speaking engagements,

vacations, sabbaticals, and anything else that should be understood in an open, responsible Christian relationship.

Working accords should be sufficiently elastic to accommodate change, creativity, and the prompting of the Holy Spirit, but sufficiently binding to dispel uncertainty and to free all parties to work at a high level of efficiency and love. Agreements should be periodically reviewed and altered where needed.

Unless you and your fellow members demonstrate genuine credibility, the work of your pastor will be extremely difficult, if not impossible. However skilled and consecrated, no minister can accomplish anything in the church single-handedly. By definition and design it must be a mutual ministry; each must draw upon the other. The pastor inherits the good and less desirable attributes of your congregation. He becomes a part of your ministry, and you a part of his witness. Together you offer your stewardship of love and service to God.

Following procedures authentic to your denomination and congregation, you called your minister to come live and work with you. Just as you were proud of his conduct during the courtship, now that the marriage is consummated, may he be as proud of your openness and dependability.

As a rule, a community is no better than its churches. Churches seldom exceed the vision and vitality of their pastors. And ministers are no better than their training and support. Be proud of your minister. He loves you!

Jesus conceptualized the mutual ministry of a parish when he said, "Whoever would be great among you must be your servant, and whoever would be first among you must be your slave; even as the Son of man came not to be served but to serve, and to give his life as a ransom for many" (Matt. 20:26b–28).

YOUR CALL

We have been discussing some of the methods and experiences by which individuals find their Christian vocation. Our concern has focused primarily on the pastor. We have endeavored to show that, to a degree unknown to many, he is conscious of a presence, aware of a power that has emancipated him, freed him, to minister.

You, too, have been called to serve Christ. Although your training and vocational setting vary from that of your minister, like him, if your faith and tolerance, spirit and love do not resemble those qualities of life associated with Jesus, you qualify as "a noisy gong or a clanging cymbal" (1 Cor. 13:1).

4

His Sermons

"My last pulpit committee meeting," wrote a perceptive churchman, "was the *coup de grace.*" The suave chairman, an attorney, advised the prospective minister being interviewed, "We're tired of hearing troubling sermons. We want someone who'll make us feel good on Sunday morning."

Is it the purpose of a sermon to make worshipers feel good? Good for what, for whom? At times the message should be soothing. But not as a steady diet.

Do you want your minister to be a soothsayer, a spiritual masseur, who touches sensitive issues so lightly there is no pain nor personal association with guilt?

Do you want your preacher to be such a connoisseur and peddler of words that you are so mesmerized by his cleverness and beautiful ambiguity that you leave corporate worship unconvinced, unchanged, and unchallenged?

Is not a Christian sermon supposed to comfort the distressed and disturb the comfortable and complacent?

Is the sermon just a synopsis of the pastor's weekly reading, or is it his earnest interpretation of Scripture pertinent to today's living?

WHAT IS A SERMON?

There is a difference between an oration and a sermon; a speech and a sermon. There is precise distinction between a good speaker and a good preacher. A good preacher is a good speaker, but the latter is not necessarily a preacher! An orator is so endowed with mind, voice, grace, and vocabulary that he can address himself to a spate of subjects acceptably and persuasively without involving himself or his audience. Although the preacher strives to perfect the art of speaking, he is more than a Winston Churchill with words. He is—and must forever be—a John the Baptist crying in the contemporary wilderness: "Prepare the way of the Lord, make his paths straight" (Mark 1:3b).

Regardless of preparation or theological persuasion, the preacher must communicate God's love as revealed by Jesus in clear, convincing language. The man in the pulpit must be so confident of his calling, so acquainted with Christ, that he will be able to say to his peers: "I know Jesus Christ better than any man in this room."

A sermon is always the articulation of the preacher's spiritual acumen; the bottom line of his declaration of faith; a fresh and stirring presentation on the coming, the ministry, and the presence of Christ. As Richard Baxter proclaimed, the minister must preach "as a dying man to dying men."

A public speaker is tutored in the techniques of communication and acquainted with popular concerns and conditions of a given community. He is careful to orchestrate prejudice to articulate what his audience pays to hear. If he has a reputation, he is more likely booked through an agent who determines appearances and fees.

The preacher's approach and credentials are different. No one is more concerned over general conditions, and few are better informed than the alert pastor. His expertise and orientation exceed the requirements of the lecture circuit.

The minister is a spokesman for God! He is not sponsored by any segment of the community or power base. The fee does not determine his style or language. It is true that a congregation pays the pastor that he *may* preach; he is not paid *to* preach. By nature his mission and ordination make him a world citizen. His pastorate is without frontiers.

Your minister is God's agent of reconciliation. He is not only convinced of the relevancy, power, and place of preaching in a decadent society; he is a sermon read by everyone along Main Street.

The preacher is more than an actor; the sermon more than a well-rehearsed drama. While the message is not a dramatic play, it should be biblically conceived, artistically arranged, and esoterically irresistible. C. S. Lewis saw a sermon as more than a series of propositions offered for acceptance, but as an appeal "sent from God."

The survival of the sermon through the ages is evidence of its divine origin and intended purpose. When the sermon is viewed as a relic to be revered and preserved, or as a historic re-

minder of apostolic procedures, or a time-frame
to be filled in the order of Sunday worship, its
disillusionment is inevitable.

A sermon is not a religious hangover that fad-
dish forms of worship can dismiss. It is not
a religious recitation carefully rehearsed for
public consumption. Nor is it a soliloquy; or a
monologue skillfully modulated in a sanctuary
suffused with sacred music.

A sermon is a dialogue—a sacrament of words
and convictions articulated in love and hope.
A sermon is not intended for listening only, but
also to stimulate action. The preacher asks for
a verdict! The great British statesman William
E. Gladstone maintained that a good speaker
was one who had the ability "to send back in
copious streams what the people send up to him
in mist." This is precisely true of what takes
place between the pulpit and the pew. Together
they create a sermon!

SERMONS CHANGE LIVES

We are impressed not only by the survival
of the sermon across the ages, but also by its
impact on human responses. The well-con-
ceived, well-delivered sermon has transforming
power. From Paul preaching before Felix, gov-
ernor of Judaea, to your pastor at his best, minds
have been changed, hearts softened, souls saved.
Every experienced pastor has remembrances of
individuals whose responses to his sermons were
unforgettable.

As a strong believer in the accountability of
accumulated possessions, a practitioner of tithing as a biblical approach to responsible Chris-

tian stewardship, I preach often on this aspect
of our faith, not just at budget time. How well
I remember the Sunday in a metropolitan pulpit, when, after preaching on "Tipping or Tithing?," I felt moved to extend an invitation for
those who would like to test the biblical admonition to tithe. The Lord must have approved,
for fifty serious Christians came forward to register as conscientious stewards. Many interesting,
measurable, and lasting consequences resulted.

Shortly thereafter a businesswoman, active in
the life of the church, came to my study to express appreciation for the challenge to demonstrate Christian credibility in the use of time,
talent, and treasure. During the course of her
visit, she volunteered, "I have just disposed of
a $20,000 property. I am giving the church a
tithe of it. Do you have any suggestions on how
it should be used?"

Sixteen years later, while attending a special
service in that same congregation, I was house
guest of a prominent banker. Reminiscing, he
related how my sermons on stewardship had
stimulated him to deeper dedication. Referring
to that glorious Sunday when fifty souls committed themselves to become tithers, he said, "I
was among them. At the time we had two young
children to support on a very small salary. I did
not see how we could do it, but the challenge
was irresistible. The Lord has blessed us beyond
our deserving, and I want you to know we are
still tithing."

Believe it or not, while drafting this chapter
in Florida, I encountered a former parishioner,
a much-sought-after professional man who,
when he discovered what I was doing, came
forward with this testimony.

According to my friend, I had been admonishing the brethren to demonstrate greater concern for winning people to Christ. It seems that we—the associates and I—had sent out a letter to about fifty men in this sizable, sophisticated congregation, challenging them to commit themselves to giving one night a week to evangelistic visitation.

"When the letter came," my friend reported, "I read it and thought, *That's a good idea, but there are many abler and wiser men in the church to do the work; they won't miss me.* So I wadded up the letter and threw it in the wastebasket!

"Next Sunday," he continued, "we were at church sitting in the center balcony. Again you preached on the necessity of winning people to Christ. You referred to some of the experiences you had with members of our congregation. I was uncomfortable. I felt you were preaching directly to me. On the way home I asked my wife if she had emptied the wastebasket by my desk. The answer was 'yes.'

" 'Where did you put it?'

" 'It's in the garbage can.'

"Together we rummaged through the garbage, and, down toward the bottom of the can was the letter, spotted with bacon grease. I took it out, cleaned it up the best I could, and sent it back to the church officer with an affirmative answer. Three years later I was elected chairman of our evangelistic group. . . ."

Who can assess the impact of a sermon?

A sincere sermon is prayer turned around. In the latter, we weak and wayward mortals communicate our fears and sins, our promises and hopes to God. In the former, God communicates his desires, his will to us through the miracle of preaching! Christian truth must be fleshed for most of us to see and to accept. The sermon is God's continuing conduit for the living Word.

WHAT IS PREACHING?

In the Lyman Beecher Lectures on preaching delivered before the Divinity School of Yale College in 1877, Phillips Brooks declared, "Preaching is the communication of truth by man to men. It has in it two essential elements, truth and personality."

Preaching is the fusion of the "truest truth" and the finest in human character. For the message to have credence and compulsion, it must come through the proclaimer—not merely through his pen, typewriter, or over his lips, but through every fiber of his intellectual and moral being.

Although Christian capacity, personality, skill, and spirit commingle in producing a sermon, the validity of preaching is not determined by one's position or authority. Being preordained by God, Christ is the authority and judge of all preaching. This brings us to the heart of the matter: What is preaching?

Preaching had its heroic beginnings with John the Baptist and Jesus, who came declaring that the kingdom of God was at hand; they called upon their hearers to repent and believe in the gospel. Christ's courageous pronouncements filled listeners with fear, faith, and hope. His final command was: "Go therefore and make disciples of all nations, baptizing them in the name of the Father and of the Son and of the

Holy Spirit, teaching them to observe all that I have commanded you; and lo, I am with you always, to the close of the age" (Matt. 28:19,20).

The Lord entrusted believers with the responsibility of communicating and actualizing the gospel. Preaching is the chosen instrument by which the church offers the Good News. Paul expressed it succinctly when writing to the Romans: "And how are they to hear without a preacher? And how can men preach unless they are sent?" (10:14,15).

Long ago, Robert Hall declared that "miracles were the bells of the universe which God rang to call men to hear his Son." Magnificent as have been the methods of presenting the Saving Person of Galilee, none has excelled those accomplished through the miracles of preaching.

Your pastor, a prophet and priest, is frequently so moved by the revelation and confirmation of truth found in Jesus that he lives on tiptoe, scanning the farthest boundary of his horizon; his ecstasy so intense that he is often reduced to tears. He knows what John Edgar Park meant when he said, "preaching begins with a lump in the throat."

Preaching is the delicate balance between the apprehension and the experience of truth. It is a different miracle to different people. As Professor Halford H. Luccock of Yale used to say, "Preaching is communicating the gospel."

In his book, *The Preacher's Task and the Stone of Stumbling,* D. T. Niles viewed preaching as an "invitation to the Supper. . . ." Preaching, he maintained, is set in the context of the proclaimer and the hearer, who are being saved. It must also be considered in the context of the

"Church's warfare with the world" and in "the context of the continuing ministry of Christ as the cross-bearer of the world."

David H. C. Read, minister of Madison Avenue Presbyterian Church, New York City, refers to preaching as a unique event with human words, a sacrament! The popular pulpiteer continues, "It is a sacramental mystery in which, through the power of the Holy Spirit, the 'bread and wine' of the everyday speech of very ordinary mortals become the vehicles for the Real Presence of Christ."

LABOR OF LOVE

However interpreted, preparing to preach is a labor of love; the most demanding of disciplines. It has been said that Hinduism lives by ritual, Buddhism by mystic meditation, and Confucianism by peculiar conduct, but Christianity lives and grows by the "foolishness of preaching."

One prominent pulpiteer took this aspect of his ministry so seriously that he established for himself the exhausting pattern of one hour's preparation for each minute in the pulpit.

Great preachers labor long and hard not only on their sermons, but in self-preparation. Realizing they are custodians of the riches of his grace, they are constantly being reshaped by Christ. They are never satisfied with traditional clichés and denominational slogans but forever strive to articulate the will of God for his people.

Preparation of the preacher must complement and supplement preparation of the message, the arrangement of ideas derived from Scripture and life. It was said of John Wesley

that he "set himself on fire and the people came
to see him burn."

HELP YOUR MINISTER PREACH

It is quite possible that your pastor is a better
preacher than his sermons indicate. He must
have time to study and meditate. He cannot be
janitor of the church, errand boy, offer the invo-
cation or benediction at every community function to which he is invited, and still have time
to discover and communicate God's will.

Preachers make churches, and churches make
preachers. One obvious place where this asser-
tion is actualized is when a congregation says
to its pastor, "Look, we have called you to lead
us into a greater understanding of the Christian
faith; arrange your schedule, study and prayer
habits to allow ample time for personal communion and growth. You are our spiritual leader!
We want to share this ministry with you. Let
us relieve you of routine chores and unrea-
sonable assignments. Tell us what should be
done. . . ."

This happened to me early in my ministry.
Following worship one Sunday, a brilliant attorney a few years my senior said in the gentlest
kind of way, "Remember, pastor, we have about
100 people at church to hear you preach. This
aggregates more than 5,000 man hours per year.
That's a lot of time. Make it worthwhile."

Even though he assured me I was doing acceptably, I was not prepared for such a comment. His conversation concluded with this
challenge: "If I—or the congregation—can help
you reach your potential, let us know."

From that friendly encounter, gradually a

concept of mutual ministry emerged which continues to this day. That small congregation set the pattern for my ministry by seeing to it that I had a pleasant place to study, adequate salary, vacation and travel experiences to renew my mind and spirit. Members of the church assisted in developing a responsible schedule, respected my disciplines, and, except in cases of emergencies, I was seldom disturbed during study time. Preaching in that pulpit was an event!

You can do as much for your minister. Begin by having a few dedicated members meet with him at breakfast, lunch, or in some informal setting: discuss "the state of the church." Discover his feelings toward the community, the congregation; listen for his frustrations and irritations, his needs and expectations. Assure him of your friendship and support. Listen when your pastor bares his soul. Determine proper starting points for the correction of problems and the initiation of programs. Free him of miscellaneous chores, encourage him to become the best preacher in the community.

Having made these suggestions, you should be prepared to live with change and expense. He may need a more adequate study or library. Then again, he may be overworked. It could be he needs an assistant or a better secretary. The war department of the church—the choir—may be driving him crazy. Help him organize for a more responsible and productive ministry. Form a small committee to serve as buffer, to absorb shocks from the congregation and the community.

Neither advertise nor ignore your pastor's weaknesses; help him overcome them.

ARE YOU EXPECTING TOO MUCH?

At a relatively young age I was called to succeed a prominent pulpiteer. In my denomination his name was synonymous with the cultural city where he ministered. Although proud of the opportunity and grateful for the confidence exhibited by this prestigious congregation, I was nevertheless apprehensive. Whatever the duty at hand, I was enveloped by the enormous shadow of my illustrious predecessor. He was gracious, exceedingly considerate and cooperative. His counsel was invaluable. He was one of the best listeners on Sunday. And, as was my custom, when I rewrote the sermon on Monday, he usually wanted to read it. He wrote a flattering introduction to my first book of sermons. Even so, I was uneasy and constantly asking my wife and myself, "How am I doing? Am I measuring up to expectations?"

During this prolonged period of adjustment I encountered a friend whose counsel brought great stability to my ministry. There was in the community a fine university with a school of religion where I taught a course in homiletics. One day after class, while I was visiting with a professor of Old Testament, a Yale Ph.D., a splendid Chrisitan, he asked, "How are things going at the church?" This was followed by a more direct question: "How is your preaching?" as if he sensed my struggle.

Having known him for a number of years, I unburdened my heart. Afterwards he sympathetically stated, "Let me say to you what I say to my pastor; namely, if he brings six great sermons a year, I'm satisfied."

Not every layman is so perceptive, so aware of the involvements and demands of preaching. His wisdom has stood me in good stead.

HELP HIM RING THE BELL

Preaching, as we have seen, is strenuous. No one can possibly ring the miracle bell for God every time he stands up to preach. Yet I find a nervous impatience among many congregations with their minister if he does not "deliver" Sunday after Sunday according to preconceived ideas of preaching. Some self-appointed judges expect their pastor "to hit a home run" every time he goes to the plate—the pulpit! It is impossible! Not even the kings of baseball—Ruth, Maris, and Aaron—could do it.

You, the officers and members of the congregation, can be a source of inspiration and strength to your pastor by constantly encouraging him. Find something you liked or needed in the Sunday sermon and thank him for it, not just in your comment as you leave but in a thoughtful memo or phone call a day or two later. Protect him from undue criticism and impossible working conditions.

If the congregation insists that the mimeographing be done in the "so-called" pastor's study, mailings go out from his office, church literature be distributed between "Sunday school" and morning worship, then don't complain about his sermons, for he hasn't had a chance! You will not find a surgeon operating in a hospital cafeteria or a judge passing out political propaganda as persons enter his court.

Don't expect your pastor to be a memory bank at the door following worship. Don't ask him questions that require specific dates and times when circumstances will not permit detailed answers or when the church calendar is far removed. Instead, hand him a written note.

The pastor's study should be a special place. It does not have to be plush to be private and attractive. However, it does need to be spacious, inviting, and comfortable. Studying the blueprints of my first building program, a seasoned church architect said, "Don't skimp on your study; you can't think and develop great thoughts in a closet."

As a professing Christian and as a member of the congregation that called your pastor, it is incumbent upon you to know him. There is only one of him but many of you for him to know. You will discover his humanity, charity, and gratitude for your concern and friendship. In the privacy of his study share with him the needs of the congregation as you see them, as well as those of your own household. Raise questions concerning aspects of the Christian faith that trouble or encourage you. In this way you will not only develop a friend, but contribute to your pastor's arsenal of ideas and knowledge without telling him what to preach.

Joseph Parker, a physical and spiritual giant, was the powerful preacher of City Temple, London, from 1869 to 1902. Among his last words to a friend were: "Keep up the pulpit!"

BETWEEN TWO WORLDS

Despite the distorted images of the minister and his complex role in a computerized society, he is nevertheless a visible symbol and frequently an effective voice between two worlds.

He has heard the drums of destiny, and he is leading the march toward heaven.

One is reminded of a dramatic story concerning King George V. In the later years of his reign, it was customary for him to broadcast an annual message to the empire. During one of these broadcasts, when the ears of the world were waiting to hear the voice of the king, an alert engineer in the radio studio noticed that an important wire was broken. America was cut off! Suddenly, as if nudged by an angel, a perceptive mechanic seized the broken wires and, holding one in each hand, completed the circuit, thus enabling America to hear the king.

In the broken and frightening connections of our world, how can the Word of the Lord be heard unless it passes through the preacher—your preacher? And how can the message be received and implemented without hearers and doers?

5

His Emotional Load

A placard, used in recruiting priests, read:
"The great moments in a person's life are:

> Birth
> Confirmation
> Communion
> Marriage
> Death

Would you like to be the person
Most needed at such times?"

Although these irretrievable moments in life's pilgrimage require great skill and understanding, they are by no means the only events that emotionally drain the minister.

The conscientious servant of the Lord also wants to be near when Johnny fails to make the varsity; when pregnancy forces unwed Mary to quit school; when, after thirty years of apparent happiness, Tom and Betty file for a divorce; when Louis is depressed because he did not get the anticipated promotion; when Gilbert marries outside his church and culture; when Elizabeth is committed to an institution; when prolonged illness and medical expenses compel the Browns to sell their home; when Leonard, the only son, is killed in a highway accident; when Margaret is ready for college but there is no money! These and countless other recurring situations tug at the minister's heart, causing fitful sleep.

UNLIMITED EXPOSURE

No one is more pleased or perplexed by life's surprises and heartbreaking sorrows than the concerned pastor. His is a constant exposure to human turbulence. It is not uncommon for a minister to conduct a funeral, a wedding, have a hospital emergency, a church conference, demanding correspondence, and a rash of disturbing telephone calls within a single twelve-hour day. Although trained in such matters, the sensitive servant cannot immediately wash his mind and heart of the day's deposits and duress.

The question is: How can your pastor continue to offer encouragement and comfort to people day after day? What saves him from becoming perfunctory and pontifical? Since it is difficult to minister to illness out of illness, to the distressed out of frustration, how is the minister to maintain his equilibrium, health, and contagious spirituality?

Like all who wish to live intelligently and helpfully, the pastor must have an understanding of what is involved in human emotions. As early as 1884, William James defined emotion as "a state of mind that manifests itself by sensible changes in the body."

The human brain is the control tower. This

pinkish-gray mass is about the size of a softball, weighing approximately three pounds. Although it is exceedingly complicated, an ingenious switchboard of instantaneous commands and responses, the human brain is the sensitive organ of adjustment. Its voluntary and involuntary activity is phenomenal. We experience some kind of emotion every minute. Changes take place in muscles, blood vessels, viscera, and the endocrine glands. These physical and chemical changes, together with the mental state that accompanies them, comprise emotion.

Emotions are produced through the autonomic nervous system and the glands. Generally speaking, they may be classified as "unpleasant" and "pleasant." Overstimulation of any organ or muscle produces unpleasantness and frequently pain. Anger, anxiety, fear, apprehension, and sorrow are examples of excess stimulation. Pleasant emotions are usually more "optional," less extreme in nature, and briefer in duration. We recognize such manifestations in expressions of joy, comfort, cooperation, affection, and sex.

Located inside the cranium and beneath the brain is the pituitary gland. It is said to be no larger than a green pea, yet this powerful little generator produces a variety of hormones involved in raising and lowering the blood pressure and regulating muscular coordination. The chemistry and climate of the body are constantly changing. Sometimes these changes are so violent that irresponsibility and illness result, even death.

One night at a banquet table my neighbor said, "I had a horrible experience this week."

He proceeded to tell about his boss, a fine man, possessed by a "beastly temper," who literally dropped dead in his office following a heated argument.

COPING WITH PSYCHE

Less discernible, though equally dangerous, is the quiet, day-by-day drip, drip of a gland on an imaginary, exaggerated, or real problem. Eventually the emotional strain will induce illness. In fact, the vast majority of our physical problems may be tied up with emotional disturbances. Interestingly enough, instead of superior minds being immune to emotionally induced conflicts and diseases, they seem to be more susceptible.

The minister seeks to understand the miracle, function, and destiny of man. Moreover, he knows that every person is physically, mentally, and emotionally tuned to a very fine tolerance. Thus, the pastor will be sympathetic and gentle in dealing with individuals, having heeded the English divine of the seventeenth century, Jeremy Taylor, who admonished his colleagues to "speak kindly to all, for every man has a problem."

Love is more than religious idealism. It is an indispensable emotion; the Christian prescription for fruitful living.

Every person is a complicated biological phenomenon filled with such powerful impulses and drives as dependence, self-love, competitiveness, envy, hostility, sexuality, and fear. The fulfillment of these hungers determines the strength and attractiveness of personality. When a person is insecure, holds grudges, or is inadequately loved, he usually demonstrates hostility in one form or another. Subsequently, a strange interaction of neglected love and hostility occurs. The ego is inflated and irritated. The victim of such formidable forces usually becomes increasingly aggressive or regressive. The minister must be acquainted with the dynamics of personality if he would effectively serve and safeguard his own health.

Moreover, your spiritual shepherd realizes that some individuals can endure more pressure, disappointment, and pain than others. Human beings are more than chemical combinations; they are extremely complex and different from each other, except, perhaps, identical twins. So-called well-adjusted people may not be equally intelligent, physically well-endowed, or talented. We are not created equal! It takes all kinds to make up the world—and many kinds are found in every church.

Your perceptive pastor, through counseling sessions, visits, and from the pulpit endeavors to shed light on personal "hang-ups" and leave deposits of love.

HELP SAVE YOUR PREACHER

If the minister would bear his burdens and enable others to bear theirs, he must understand his role. He is God's agent of reconciliation, not a judge; an enabler, not a debater. Although tempted at times to play God, the preacher also has feet of clay and needs encouragement.

Like all high-strung, sensitive souls, clerics are prime candidates for breakdowns. They are especially vulnerable to disorders and diseases re-

lated to emotional involvements, tensions, and
anxiety. Like heavily laden vehicles, clergy must
stop periodically to evaluate their load: to see
if they are becoming workaholics—whether personal concerns are too overwhelming. At these
way stations laity and clergy need to confer—
intentionalize and verbalize their mutual ministry.

How, then, can you and your pastor experience and share the Christian pilgrimage with
maturity, mutual respect, and supportiveness?
How can you preserve one another's sanity?
How can stereotyped images of the minister be
dispelled?

Consider these comments on saving your
preacher:

1. *Why do you need a minister?*

You believe in the priesthood of believers, and
you are a believer; why a preacher? I raised
this question with a group of lay persons during
a dialogue following a sermon. Quickly a suave
lawyer replied, "To do for the church what we
busy laymen don't have time to do." His unin-
formed concept of the minister was that of a
hired man; he implied pastors are not busy. If
for no other reason, clergy are needed to keep
the Christian ministry in perspective, to interpret and demonstrate Christ's mission, to remind people of God. Tensions are eased,
conflicts minimized when congregations and
clergy mutually explore and define expectations
and performances.

2. *You can help liberate your pastor from de-nominational captivity and from unreasonable,*

if not un-Christian, congregational and community demands.

The minister is so programmed that the search and struggle for identity and acceptance are greatly intensified. Denominational adjudicators and benevolent bureaucrats are too involved in church structure, competition, conferences and statistics to minister to your perplexed pastor. Humanly speaking, perceptive, supportive laity are the last hope for ministering to ministers. Be a pastor to your pastor!

3. *Your minister is probably underpaid.*

Although pastoral salaries have escalated in the last decade, they are still lower than in other sectors of society. Programmed to believe that "the love of money is the root of evil," and it probably is, the average minister has been naive and timid about his compensation. He has felt it was inappropriate to negotiate terms of employment. While this sad stereotype is rapidly disappearing, much of the confusion persists because it emerged from the Protestant ethos of a rural society. It has not been sufficiently challenged or corrected. Pastors have been slow to organize themselves for responsible support and negotiation. If psyche compensation was ever adequate, it is woefully inadequate today.

Don't push your pastor to "moonlight" to balance his family budget.

Money is not what it was a few generations ago. It is still power, a commodity, the medium of exchange, but it is also the affirmation of expectation and the confirmation of acceptance. Corporate executives know the value of bonuses, fringe benefits, dividends from travel, and leisure time. Money can be an extension of concern, a definition of values, measurable love.

Save your pastor from becoming a professional parasite, a shopper who feels obliged to ask for a clergy discount or who is solicitous in the presence of affluence.

Do not permit your minister to become a suave chiseler!

4. *Another anomaly peculiar to the minister which overstimulates the adrenalin is the work schedule.*

The majority of civil servants in your community, regardless of station, have far more time off than does your pastor. By necessity, clergy must work when others are lounging in leisure: holidays, nights, and weekends. Add this to the normal workload, and it is not uncommon for servants of the church to average sixty to eighty hours a week. This is too much! It is partly the minister's fault. He has been too willing to accept traditional patterns of operating the church. I am guilty. I once moved from a congregation which gave its minister a vacation of six weeks to one that granted only three weeks. Although I worked hard to make a church out of what I inherited, no one ever suggested a longer vacation, and I was too proud to ask for it.

5. *Another annoying practice in many churches—and one which brings on illness—is the exclusion of the preacher from participation in decision-making processes.*

Ruling bodies of the church desire his input, yes, but not always the weight of his voice. In fact, the structure of some churches denies him the right to vote. While he is usually considered and accepted as the titular head of the congregation, present in the role of an ex-officio member of commissions and committees, voting and manipulation of influence are done by others. Such discrimination and independent decisions frequently result in delicate, even impossible, working relationships.

6. *Undue pride can be a deterrent to the minister and his people.*

Such a stance increases the emotional load.

Humility is an unmistakable mark of maturity. Any hostility directed against the overly proud individual wounds the ego and results in various forms of retaliation. Like scrappy soldiers, the white blood cells rush forward at the slightest indication of invasion to preserve the body's health. Just so, an enormously fresh supply of pride surges to the surface in moments of conflict to preserve the ego. Hostility breeds hostility. Pride multiplies until the victim creates a perverted picture of himself.

The sincere Christian acknowledges he is not an authority in all fields. Yet some churchmen have a propensity for posing as experts in areas foreign to their training and experience. Furthermore, the mature disciple knows that relevant questions are more important than dogmatic answers. St. Augustine knew this and commented, "The sufficiency of my merit is to know that my merit is not sufficient."

7. *Help your congregation update its concept of individual and corporate ministry; help it comprehend the pastor's internalizing of priori-*

ties; encourage members to appreciate the hu-
manity of their spiritual leader.

Refine and publicize congregational goals. Periodically review agreements with your church
staff, thus reducing anxiety and indifference.
Genuine concern and common courtesy will
greatly reduce the emotional *load* of your pastor.

SENSITIVE SOULS AND SUICIDE

As a young man, Leo Tolstoy, utterly discouraged, flirted with suicide. Once Mark Twain put
a pistol to his head but could not pull the trigger.
Suicide also challenged William James. Abraham
Lincoln walked the brink of insanity following
the death of Anne Rutledge.

American churchmen were shocked to learn
of a suicide pact between Dr. and Mrs. Henry
Pitney Van Dusen. On January 28, 1975, they
took overdoses of sleeping pills. She died
quickly, but he vomited up the pills, was found
and taken to a hospital where he eventually died
of a heart attack.

Who was Henry Van Dusen? He was the retired president of Union Theological Seminary,
New York City. This distinguished Presbyterian
minister and scholar was one of my favorite
preachers. It was my privilege to know him and
to drive him across Missouri on one occasion.

The Van Dusens felt individuals were entitled
to euthanasia. They had discussed what form
of exit they should take from this world. Now
they were old and ailing. Mrs. Van Dusen was
eighty, her husband seventy-seven. Their brief

note stated that they hoped their act would not be misunderstood or hurt anyone too much. "We are both increasingly weak and unwell, and who would want to die in a nursing home?"

Such sad experiences should compel the Christian community to reevaluate its responsibility for and relationship to spiritual leaders.

A prominent pulpiteer shared what it was like to reach the "pit of utter despair," and the temptation to slit his throat with a razor. With candid frankness, he spoke of days spent in a sanitarium at Elmira, New York. His condition, like that of many a minister, was not caused by overwork, but sheer joy! "It was not trouble that slew me, but happiness—the excitement of the most exhilarating opportunity I had ever had."

As senior minister of a famous church in New York City, he was later able to identify with all kinds of human frailties. Frequently during counseling sessions with a person suffering from obsessive anxiety, he would interrupt to say, "Don't you tell me, let me tell you how you feel." The frustrated individual would exclaim, "I can't believe it! How did you know that?"

He had been there.

SELF PORTRAIT

How well I remember the rigors and romances of my first parish, a congregation of eighty souls. Everything was a challenge, from learning to heat water on a laundry stove to preaching without notes! With utter abandonment, I gave myself to the church, night and day. I preached at the county jail with regularity, as well as at convict camps along highways. The pulpit was portable.

Taking a tip from the early years of another's ministry, I would not permit a telephone in my study, and, despite the fact that I was a one-man staff, I disciplined myself to study at least three hours a day. Although I still had some of the bounce and stamina of an athlete, after two years of constant driving, I became so "uptight" I could not sleep. At night I would lie awake, reliving the encounters of the day, anticipating the excitement of tomorrow.

Gradually, I began to lose weight; I became nervous and developed ulcers. Finally, my physician said, "Perhaps you should give up the ministry. You are too conscientious and highstrung." That was the blow which eventually brought me to my senses. I was forced to discipline myself—to become more democratic in operating the church. During those tedious years of redirecting energy, I had ample opportunity to test the validity of the ageless rhythms of life as advocated by the late Arnold J. Toynbee: namely, "thrust" and "retardation."

I learned, as indeed everyone must, that one cannot stay forever on the firing line. One must retreat now and again to gain perspective, recoup, and replenish self. It is more therapeutic to learn from one's wounds than to lick them!

KEEPING WELL

The physical health of preachers will compare favorably with that of other persons. Insurance companies consider ministers good risks. But what of their emotional health?

Psychiatrists suggest that emotional health and maturity are virtually synonymous. While the terms are not as easily defined as those employed to describe visible maladies, maturity is generally conceived to indicate the emotional development of an individual. This is a continual process, usually coinciding with one's inner awareness of himself and his motivation. It requires more than sheer brain power to control certain emotional responses. Frequently one's conduct is traceable to trouble within, perhaps extending back to some childhood experience. An adequate understanding and demonstration of maturity are essential to the minister's ability to satisfactorily perform daily responsibilities.

Immaturity is a continuing characteristic of the race. Much of our grief, anxiety, and frustration stem from immaturity. It does not always coincide with age but always with attitude! Sigmund Freud believed that psychological maturity excluded religious dimensions. To him life could only be understood in terms of motivational forces. Carl Jung, the Swiss physician, claimed that "the spiritual quest is essentially an attempt to become what we were meant to be."

Although a baby attracts more attention and affection than most celebrities, nothing is more obnoxious or repulsive than an adult who refuses to grow up.

Like all people, clergy must learn to live with themselves and with others. Their emotional load is inescapable. Unlike other persons in the community, they are familiar with the valleys of sorrow, mountains of transfiguration, and the drab ruts of daily monotony. Each appointment

and service, person and problem, initiates costly
choices and decisive decisions.

ON CONSTANT CALL

When an engaged couple seeking marital
counsel sits before your minister, he has no time
to consult experts. The lovers have come out
of respect and hope that this designated servant
of God may be able to make their marriage more
meaningful. Months later, when their first child
is born dead, the pastor must share their loss
and encourage them to "recapture the rapture"
that prepared them for this anticipated event.

When a sobbing voice from the hospital calls
at two o'clock in the morning saying, "John has
gone; would you please come over?" there is
no time for procrastination and precious little
for preparation. Weeping with those who weep
wrings dry a preacher's soul!

When a stranger, in the privacy of the pastor's
study, confesses his sins and asks for prayer and
guidance, your minister has no time or intention
of holding a summit conference to evaluate the
man's sincerity. He must respond. The minister
does what he can to assist the visitor in experi-
encing forgiveness, inciting courage to begin
again.

When a member meets with an accident, or
suddenly experiences some devastating rever-
sal, or "stumbles into paradise," the minister is
an understanding participant in these transforming events.

However demanding and enervating the day,
when the church program is sagging, whispering
campaigns audible, people indifferent to opportunity and officers of the congregation derelict

in duty, facilities and budget inadequate, the pastor must act. He must discover and demonstrate a way of life conducive to and commensurate with his high calling.

DAYTIGHT COMPARTMENTS

In 1913 Sir William Osler delivered the Silliman Lectures at Yale. In the course of an erudite address, the noted British physician compared life to a sea voyage and man to a mighty ship. He urged his audience to go to the bridge and examine the working order of the bulkheads, and to make certain that the doors of the past were securely shut and those of the future were not left ajar. Dr. Osler admonished the students to live in daytight compartments. "The load of tomorrow, added to that of yesterday, carried today, makes the strongest falter." Jesus put it this way, "Therefore do not be anxious about tomorrow, for tomorrow will be anxious for itself. Let the day's own trouble be sufficient for the day" (Matt. 6:34).

This is not a philosophy of laissez-faire or resignation. Neither is it intended to suppress ambition and freedom, but simply to remind us again and again that the present is all that we have. We possess the past through memory and the future by anticipation.

Learning to live one day at a time is our paramount assignment. Too many of us try to live a week at a time, a month, or a year! While planning is essential to happiness and effectiveness, the present is our privilege. Thomas Carlyle's counsel is pertinent: "Our main business is not to see what lies dimly at a distance, but to do what lies clearly at hand."

6
His Family

"Can Carter Revitalize the American Family?"

Deputy Editor of *U. S. News and World Report* George E. Jones reacted to this question in the February 28, 1977 issue.

Although we are grateful for our president's concern and his faith in the primacy of the home, contagious resurgence and unity are quite beyond his power to bestow. He may revamp laws, add new ones, juggle incomes, improve working conditions and school systems, but only homemakers—by the grace of God and the inspiration of love—can produce the miracle so desperately needed.

HAS THE FAMILY A FUTURE?

Long before Mr. James Earl Carter, Jr., gained occupancy of the White House, thoughtful individuals were asking: "Does the family have a future?"

Does the family have a future when 40 percent of America's working force are women, one-third of whom are married? Can the family survive when thousands of children come home every day from school to empty houses, baby-sitters, or written directions about preparing the evening meal? One out of six school-age Americans now lives with a single parent.

At least 1,000,000 teen-agers run away from home every year. What a commentary on American parenthood!

A national survey indicates that about 2.2 million American children between three and seventeen years of age have been "beaten up" by their parents. Annually there are at least 2,000 reported deaths from child abuse. There is no way of knowing the number of unreported fatalities, near-deaths, permanent injuries, and psychological scars inflicted.

Does the American family, once as strong as the log cabin that housed it, have a chance when media suggest its choices of products and values; project successful images; when violence is pumped into our homes under the guise of entertainment? What can we expect from idle children too young to work lawfully, yet too old to play in the confines of city lots and streets?

It is claimed that by the time an American child graduates from high school he may have watched 15,000 hours of television but has had only 11,000 hours of formal education. This is shocking! There were 624 Sundays in that span of time. Assuming church school classes averaged thirty minutes per Sunday, over the twelve-year period church pupils would have had 300 hours of Christian education. This is a generous statistic, since babies do not go to classes!

What is happening to our children?

The home, once the cement of our culture, the bulwark of ethics and morals, has become little more than a roadhouse where we change outfits hurriedly on the way to the next appointment; where premarital and extramarital sex relations are increasing, the work ethic disappearing, and Sunday has degenerated into sports day!

Divorces have increased 521 percent since 1890. Currently one out of three marriages ends in divorce; thousands of disgruntled parents live in estrangement. The Census Bureau reports that 660,000 unmarried couples are living together in our country. The number has doubled since 1970. What a picture of America!

In *Brave New World,* the Aldous Huxley's prophecy concerning promiscuity and easy dissolution of marriage seems pertinent if not fulfilled. He envisioned a day when marriage licenses could be bought like dog licenses for a specific period of time "with no lawsuit against changing dogs or keeping more than one animal at a time."

Are we approaching this point in our country?

THE PREACHER'S HOME

Fortunate is the man who is happily married. Professor William Lyon Phelps of Yale declared that a man happily married was a success, regardless of his failures in other endeavors.

In his autobiography, *As I See It,* J. Paul Getty asks this profound question: "How and why is it that I have been able to build my own automobile, drill oil wells, run an aircraft plant, build and head a business empire—yet remain unable to maintain even one satisfactory marital relationship?" His record? Five marriages and five divorces.

Irrespective of difficulties presented by our decadent society, most parishioners expect the preacher's home to be different, perfect, as if some guardian angel sat on the gatepost of the manse keeping the family safe and comfortable, relevant and religious.

Temptations of secular culture have not "passed over" the parsonage. Its occupants are well acquainted with the distractions, complexities, and challenges of the real world. Even though the vast majority of ministers' marriages are stable, divorce is not uncommon among clergy. In fact, it is increasing at a regrettable rate. Some ministers have drinking problems; some are lazy; some are power-poachers; others have poor credit or poor health. Still others are handicapped by unpredictable wives and problem children.

THE MINISTER'S WIFE

The day of "hiring two for the price of one"—meaning minister and wife, "the two-person career"—is rapidly receding into history. However, stereotypes continue. Pulpit search committees still ask pertinent questions concerning the pastor's spouse, her background, personality, and church activities. Profile placement papers circulated from denominational headquarters carry a query or two relative to the supportiveness of the preacher's wife. This will always be appropriate as a means of determining if the minister under consideration has a stable family life.

No other public servant needs a stronger home base than the minister. Like the physician, his profession is apt to impose itself on the family, and indeed, take precedence over it; his schedule is subject to sudden demands and prolonged emergencies. His days are long, and a work-week of sixty to seventy hours is typical. He needs the support, openness, and love of a family. Ministers who, through their own choice or uncontrollable circumstances, are forced to go it alone have my admiration and affection; I wonder to whom they unburden themselves.

Although I detest the subtlety and cheapness of employing a minister because his wife's talents complement, supplement, and sometimes exceed his own, I nevertheless believe that, of all professions, the ministry is a family profession! If occupants of the manse do not provide a commendable model for Christian living, the pastor is in trouble—and so is the congregation!

A single person cannot possibly comprehend the demands that a family makes on a preacher.

This is not to suggest that the occupants of the manse must be at the beck and call of every parishioner, but their visible togetherness, vitality, mutual admiration, and support become contagious. For instance, we have five sons, including two sets of twins. Even so, my wife and I managed to get the five ready for church school and morning worship. She was greatly admired and beloved because of the obvious effort involved Sunday after Sunday. Moreover, it was difficult for a lazy mother with one spoiled child to excuse herself before such an imposing example of motherhood and church involvement.

I have little patience either with wives who

nag, desert, or contribute to a divorce after entering the ministry with their husbands, or with preachers who flirt with desirable women. They should have anticipated the sacrifices, loneliness, and criticisms associated with the Christian ministry.

Following a proliferating pattern many wives of ministers are joining the thirty-five million women in today's labor market. In some instances it is an economic necessity. Others are endeavoring to escape their responsibilities. Still others want and demand to live their own lives uninhibited by the expectations of what a pastor's wife should be and do. They want freedom to be themselves, to follow professional and personal interests.

Instead of "hiring" two leaders for the price of one, now congregations face the problem of two for two! Churches must frequently find employment for the prospective pastor's wife before securing his services. This is more and more common. The wife has professional expertise, say, as a nurse, stenographer, teacher, librarian, technician. Or she has business knowledge, and she wants to be assured of employment before any commitments are made to the church. Obviously this complicates many situations. However commendable, it is difficult for the wife of a minister, mother of children, to successfully rear a family, be a teammate with her husband, and concurrently follow a personal career. I firmly believe that one of the noblest of all professions is that of housewife and mother. She stirs dreams in her children, demonstrates love, and practices faith. This is where the art of living begins.

When a prominent New York clergyman retired, his church and the City of New York honored him in many ways. As would be expected, the brilliant preacher said a number of humorous and profound things. In discussing women in the church, he lamented the fact that relatively few attained world stature in professions as compared with men. Then he smilingly said, "I know the answer. No woman has ever had a wife!" A clever and lovely way of complimenting his teammate.

A congregation called a pastor without seeing his wife. Members were shocked to discover her ethnic background. Both parties—pastor and people—were at fault. They were not open in their communications and conferences. Added to the delicate situation was the irrefutable fact that the woman seldom darkened the door of the church. I submit it is exceedingly difficult for a pastor to succeed in such a position and equally hard for parishioners to grow in grace and love.

Consider a different situation. Children of the manse are married and gone. The wife decides she'll go back to the old job or finish her degree and teach school. Economically it's fine! However, by the time she pays for someone to do the housework, spends more on clothing, purchases and maintains another car, and has the privilege of paying more taxes because of a higher income bracket, I question the economic dividends. Even so, let's assume they are satisfactory. The truth is, the women in the church miss "Mary." She is not available to talk on the telephone, and when she comes home in the evenings she is too weary to attend their meetings. As a concerned lady of an active congregation lamented, "We don't see Mary much any more since she's working."

LOVE THE CHILDREN

PK's (preachers' kids) have a different role. Saints of the parish expect them to be heavenly cherubs when, in fact, they are restless, mischievous, unpredictable little human beings. Whereas children of the manse have a remarkable achievement record in leadership and service through myriad professions and vocations, when growing up they were often victims of harsh criticism from their peers, too-high expectations from parishioners, and pressure from parents. Of all the kids in the neighborhood and at school, PK's live in a fish-bowl. They are frequently exploited, pestered, and their conduct exaggerated.

We are thankful for five sons, strong six-footers. They were a handful, a challenge, and a comfort when growing up—they still are. They were far from meek little lambs with clothes white as snow. They were boisterous boys! But we were a family; we supported one another.

We attended piano recitals, baseball, basketball, and football games, track and swim meets, wrestling matches and recognition banquets.

Six of us once drove 1,400 miles in two days to see DeWitt play against Harvard in The Game. Years later, we drove 1,000 miles to see Paul, a sophomore, start for Yale in football. Subsequently we flew halfway across the country to see Peter run in the Boston Marathon.

They have always supported their parents. When I performed the wedding ceremony for our eldest in Kentucky, a formal eight o'clock affair, it was not only emotionally strenuous, but at midnight I was leaving for an assignment in Africa. Upon arriving at the Louisville airport, there were the bride and groom to see me off!

These and other compensating experiences have increased because we have always been a family; we have endeavored to actualize the church as a family of Christians living in trust and love.

The boys accompanied us to church. It was expected. This particular parish, situated in a splendid cultural city, under the leadership of my predecessor had developed a comprehensive and compelling Thursday night dinner program. The format usually included a featured speaker, excellent music, and a brief, informal period focusing on the concerns of the church. Members were encouraged to participate— sharing an experience, telling a story. On this memorable night, Dr. Harvie Branscomb, Chancellor of Vanderbilt University, had just delivered an erudite and moving address. Questions followed. During the informal period one of our older twins, then about ten, stood up (he was a precocious child, and I feared the worst) and asked, "Dad, may I say something?"

Calling him by name, I replied, "Certainly."

"I would like to ask you people if you know what a skunk is."

There was suppressed silence.

"Well," he continued, "a skunk is a polecat with fluid drive."

Everyone howled! Needless to say, as soon as order could be restored, I dismissed the meeting. It was over but never forgotten. However, the congregation, far from chastising the lad, loved him all the more.

All of our sons were athletes in high school and college, not only because of my encouragement and interest in sports, but also because talented men in churches we served saw potential and assisted in their development.

One man, a remarkable athlete for his age, called weekly to know when he could pick up the boys for an outing, a game, or an event. There came a day when this friend brought a championship tennis racket to the parsonage. With eyes awash in tears and a voice cracking with emotion, he said to our eldest, "I want you to have this fine racket. It belonged to Charles." And who was Charles? His last son, a pilot, who was shot down over the English Channel in World War II. No amount of rhetoric could match that high moment of genuine love. The boys loved Elmer, as did the entire congregation.

Thoughtful women of the parish were equally considerate of Sybil. They not only dropped by occasionally to lend a hand with the little ones, but they also made it possible from time to time for her to have a day away from the children, even an overnight respite. Such acts of love were common and never resembled patronage.

Get acquainted with your pastor's family. You may be surprised to discover their humanity, talents, and disciplines. Wherever possible, assist in their nurture. Support activities that interest them. Drop by to see them. Sadly, a pastor told me that the chairman of his board had never been in his home. When I mentioned this to the man in question, he snapped, "He's never

been in mine, either." This is hardly the way
to build a Christian family—the church!

Samuel and Susanna Wesley had, altogether,
nineteen children; eight survived. John was the
fifteenth, Charles the eighteenth. Samuel was
an itinerant preacher. Life was hard and demanding.

Despite the lack of conveniences, no quick
means of communication or travel, no electric-
ity, no central heat, no running water, no pack-
aged foods, Susanna Wesley looked after her
household.

She expected each child to know the alphabet
by the time he was five years old. When the
children were six, she began teaching them in
the living room six hours a day: from nine to
twelve and from two to five. Think of it! Afterwards they went on to formal school, at least
two of them to Oxford.

Furthermore, she devoted one hour a day every week to each child's spiritual development.
Instead of finding excuses to stay away from
home, Susanna accepted the unique challenge
of developing Christian personalities. Is it any
wonder the Methodist Church emerged from
such a family?

Nothing so tests the resiliency of a family as
a crisis. The preacher and his loved ones are
not spared the trauma of suffering and waiting.

One Friday night—when Sunday's responsibilities were demanding attention—our eldest,
Curtis, Jr., telephoned from the nation's capital
to say DeWitt, one of the older twins, had been
involved in an automobile accident. He was in
the Yale-New Haven Hospital.

Reports indicated the young physician, going

home from work, had been hit head-on by a car. Everything seemed wrong about the collision: the driver had neither a valid license nor insurance; he was traveling at an excessive rate of speed on the wrong side of the road. Those who perpetrated the crime walked away from the scene; our son had to be cut free from his car and taken unconscious to the hospital.

For twenty-five long days and nights DeWitt remained comatose, undergoing surgery twice. While friends and relatives were wonderfully supportive, our family was at its best, the cement of love never stronger. Each son did what he could. One left heavy responsibilities to sit by his brother's bed for a week. David, 5,000 miles away, called frequently.

One night, when hope was thin, Sybil and I knelt by our bed in a room provided by a physician friend. Praying audibly, each in turn thanked God for DeWitt's life, the joy he had brought us in his academic and athletic achievements at Yale—his sense of mission and dedication to the highest. We now offered him back to God in love, asking for courage and grace to face and accept whatever the outcome.

Following our surrender to the all-wise and merciful Father, we had the best night's rest in a week. Eventually the Great Physician, together with superb and compassionate medical care, produced another miracle—the complete restoration of our son.

OPTIONS IN HOUSING

Until recently the minister has had little choice where his family would live. Churches

that could afford a full-time pastor—or a unity
of churches—provided a parsonage or manse.
As would be expected, the houses varied in ade-
quacy and comfort. Sometimes a congregation
would revamp a house to meet particular needs,
and sometimes it would not.

How well I remember the year we found ourselves living in a lovely house bought for a parsonage. It had four bedrooms on the second
floor. Our boys were small; the last set of twins,
babies. There was no lavatory on the first floor,
which meant my wife had to make countless
trips up and down the stairs taking the heavy
babies to the bathroom. Something had to be
done. As adroitly as possible I mentioned it to
the chairman of our finance committee. This
keen businessman said, "I'm sorry, but I don't
think we should spend any more money on that
place, and I won't recommend funds for a first-
floor lavatory."

This harsh decision brought Sybil to tears. Although we were borrowing money to pay a
building fund pledge and had just a few hundred
dollars in our emergency fund, we drew upon
it and had a commode installed in a closet off
the kitchen. It was a lifesaver!

Be flexible in providing housing for your pastor. Needs vary with family requirements. The
trend seems to be toward a cash monthly allow-
ance which the minister may use at his discre-
tion. Many prefer to buy their own homes.
There are obvious fiscal and tax advantages.
However, we preferred that the church provide
living quarters. Psychologically, to buy a house
while serving a church leaves the impression
the pastor is a fixture. Subsequently, he is often

taken for granted. Disposing of a house within a given time frame is sometimes difficult. Owning a home where one preaches also increases the temptation to stay on in the community after retirement, which is a mistake. The important stance is flexibility—housing that both the parish and the minister's family can live with happily. If one is not adequately housed, it adds to the stress of his ministry.

More should be involved in choosing an adequate home for the minister than sufficient square footage and the number of bathrooms. We are recommending quality housing where design and location reflect the church's stewardship and its sensitivity to pastoral needs.

Once when we were being interviewed for a prominent pulpit, the committee chairman asked my wife how she liked the manse. After a few complimentary comments on the huge monstrosity she replied, "It's a woman killer." That did it! Subsequently a functional, beautiful house was acquired. Entertaining was a pleasure. The parishioners were as proud of it as were the Joneses.

PROFILE OF A PREACHER

Our discussion here has been directed largely to the family which has the father as the minister, since about 95 percent of such families fall into this category. Yet, we gladly acknowledge and welcome women into the professional ranks of the church. Some serve as ministers' "associates" or "co-pastors" of congregations. The point I am making is this: many women ministers have home and family responsibilities, depending

upon whether they are married or single,
whether they are co-pastors with ministerial
husbands, or if they are serving separate congregations. Regardless of the professional structure
of the family occupying the manse, it is a home
of love.

A "typical" Protestant minister is male, forty-
six years old, married, and has three children.
He has graduated from college and seminary
and may have pursued additional graduate studies. His formal preparation spans at least seven
years and represents an expenditure of from
$35,000 to $50,000, depending upon the extent
and quality of his education, the majority of this
amount being paid by the student and his parents. By way of contrast, Baseball Commissioner
Bowie Kuhn says it requires $500,000 to get a
player ready for the big leagues!

The average American pastor serves a congregation of approximately 300 souls and stays less
than 5 years at a given church. The budget of
this typical parish is between $35,000 and
$40,000. According to the most recent Clergy
Support Study published by the National Council of Churches, this average pastor has an overall salary of $10,348 plus an additional $1,175
in fringe benefits. It is also reported that 14 percent of Protestant pastors earned less than
$6,000, while only 4 percent earned more than
$15,000. While salaries have increased—as
much as 50 percent in the last decade—projec-
tions are sufficiently accurate to register concern.

Moreover, according to general studies, the
average minister pays out of his own pocket
$1,134 a year in professionally related expenses.

Forty-five percent of clergy report working spouses, and 22 percent of ministers are secularly employed to supplement income.

Excluding astronomical salaries paid professional athletes, when ministerial income is contrasted with that of other professions and vocations the inequities provide shocking insights into the values of our society. According to the U. S. Department of Labor, a physician in solo practice makes approximately $50,000 a year (top specialists earn from $92,395 a year to $250,000); a dentist, $38,000; and a lawyer, $21,816. A police officer receives from $8,000–$14,000; a truck driver (local), $9,360–$11,250; long-haul, $18,300; construction electricians, $18,000; construction carpenters, $16,800; auto workers, $12,000 annually plus overtime. Many hourly workers earn $24,000.

Federal employees are well paid, with built-in step increases, generous sick leave, holidays, and vacations. According to the eighteen grades included under the General Schedule of the U. S. Civil Service Commission, a GS–5 averages $11,312 a year; a GS–10, $18,919; and a GS–15, $41,702.

Average yearly salaries of college and univ sity teachers are: instructor, $12,825; assistant professor, $13,104; associate professor, $15,290; and full professor, $20,653.

Obviously the church has not been overly generous in compensating its employees.

Dr. Carl S. Dudley, Associate Professor of Ministry, McCormick Theological Seminary, Chicago, writing in the September, 1976 issue of *The Christian Ministry,* reminds us that salary statistics do not always reflect discrepancies between compensation received by a pastor of a large church and that received by his counterpart in a small parish. Professor Dudley maintains that only one-third of Protestant congregations are financially capable of supporting a viable church program. This, he says, requires a congregation of at least 250 souls.

These sharp facts should not discourage us or serve as a deterrent, but rather as a challenge to do more for the Lord's church and those who minister in his name.

In contrast to the chairman of finance who would not permit a request of about $300 for a lavatory to go before the official board is the memory of a bank president, chairman of a splendid congregation. Twice a year during my five-year pastorate there, he would call me to his office. After exchanging pleasantries, this Lord Chesterfield in attire and grace would usually ask three questions: "How are things going at our church?" I would report as accurately as possible. "What can we do that we're not doing to strengthen the work?" If there were concerns or suggestions, I did not hesitate to mention them. He always concluded the conference with this personal query: "How are your finances? Are we paying you enough? Remember, you are our spiritual leader. You cannot lead effectively if you have financial worries."

I have been privileged to occupy prestigious pulpits, to work with a host of wonderful Christians—the majority were thoughtful—but this financier was the only one who ever took it upon himself, on a man-to-man basis, to periodically inquire about the solvency of his pastor.

HIGHER COMPENSATION

Like other public servants, ministers are becoming more effectively organized for mutual support and encouragement. A variety of parish and professional associations are emerging across the country designed to create greater negotiating leverage, bring greater understanding to ministers and their congregations.

Some hesitate to refer to the ministry as a profession. Many within its ranks are raw amateurs when it comes to dealing with church committees. There are new life styles appearing among the clergy; young men and women are less timid in articulating what the church should be doing and in voicing their own requirements for service.

At last the open negotiating process of employment has come to the church. If such negotiations are not allowed to take on the offensive and impersonal characteristics of labor and management hassles, it will be a good experience for all involved and hopefully improve the church's employment process.

Ministers are aware of a higher and more fulfilling compensation than the liberation which the paycheck brings. While they frequently deserve better working and living conditions and their salary may not be commensurate with their schooling, skills, and workloads, they are committed to assisting the Lord in building his kingdom.

Spiritual compensations are incalculable. Servants of the church are aware of their heritage and destiny. Ministers and their families live with the nitty-gritty problems of the parish.

Gossip, accidents, suffering, death, disappointments, indifference, as well as joyous experiences stipple their days. They have learned to rely on a power beyond their own, to be led, not shoved.

The vast majority of parsonage people are neither swingers nor squares, elite nor disadvantaged, but struggling human beings who feel commissioned to articulate and demonstrate the oneness which exists in Christ.

7
His Responsibilities

During a regional meeting of preachers a computer printout was distributed bearing the frightening caption: "Lost Ministers!" A well-known communion listed 152 persons who had dropped out of the ministry without leaving any information pertaining to their whereabouts or possible present employment. Officials of this denomination were soliciting assistance in finding their missing pastors.

Ministerial dropouts are common and continuing.

Your pastor, responding to a spate of church and community responsibilities, risks being buried beneath an avalanche of activities, losing sight of his mission, losing energy for his tasks, losing time for spiritual growth and communication. There is no lostness quite as pathetic as that of one so overwhelmed by agenda, expectations, and involvements that he loses enthusiasm and courage for his ministry. He becomes an empty water jug incapable of quenching life's thirst.

An exceptional preacher, sensitive to human needs, saddled with a sizeable congregation and inadequate staff, ultimately collapsed under the load. His secretary told me, when the rescue squad came to take him to the hospital, that among his last audible words were, "Now I can rest."

EDUCATOR, PHYSICIAN, SOCIAL WORKER

Like the one whom he loves and serves, Jesus Christ, your minister is a teacher. Whatever Christian instruction is needed, be it a membership class on the doctrine of the church, interpreting new denominational programs, participating in the church's school, preparing new leaders for their responsibilities, leading study and prayer groups, or instructing from the pulpit, he is always teaching. What is more important than interpreting Scripture to worshipers? Indeed, in every conversation the minister's demeanor and attitude should attempt to be contagious and inspiring. The minister is a sermon. Ralph Waldo Emerson said it well: "What you are preaches so loud that I cannot hear what you teach."

Periodically the pastor is greeted by an extrovert who seeks to magnify his image by minimizing the minister's tasks, frivolously exclaiming, "I wish I had a one-day-a-week job! Better still, one hour a week!" The laughter that follows is hollow. The exhibitionist is not funny to your exhausted pastor, who has put in a long week, much of his work going unnoticed and unreported. It may or may not reflect the reputation and health of his parish.

Neither the minister nor members should debate facetious remarks, but they should periodically respond with detailed reports of congregational and individual efforts to proper boards and committees. For his protection and the edification of the church, encourage your minister to keep comprehensive records of his work.

The preacher is a physician without pills, a surgeon without a scalpel, a lawyer without a license. This practitioner of psychology and comfort is available night and day to his parishioners—and many others—regardless of their delinquencies and circumstances. He cannot afford the protection of an unlisted telephone. Within a few hours his mind and spirit must respond to the vilest and grandest in human emotions. He must listen politely to his adversaries, and speak when silence would be less courageous. A good minister actualizes Isaiah's declaration, "Surely he has borne our griefs and carried our sorrows . . ." (53:4).

Frequently your pastor must assume the role of an unauthorized social worker investigating conditions under which many of society's forgotten souls live. He goes into the ghetto, not to gain data for politicians or public media, but as a sensitive shepherd seeking the lost, attempting to minister to individuals. This is tedious and time-consuming, and can be dangerous as well.

ADMINISTRATOR

Seminaries offer minimum training in church administration, and few pastors are privileged to attend Harvard's famous sessions for top executives. Your minister is expected to oversee, if

not personally direct, staff personnel, to create
and corollate programs. The larger the congregation, the more demanding are the administra-
tive responsibilities. As is the case with the
president of a corporation, regardless of organizational structure, praise seldom drifts back to
its source, but breakdowns in plans and communications do. Ultimately the pastor is held responsible for every aspect of the church's
witness and work. An awesome thought!

Organizational refinement has been popular
for the past few decades. "The organizational
man" is mirrored in every institution and nowhere more visibly than in the church. Much
camouflage reorganization is designed to control
society, a particular branch of government, or
an institution. Unlike normal management control, church administration is not intended to
protect the status quo, exploit workers, or increase profits. While the intelligent pastor is familiar with the dynamics of action and knows
what motivates individuals, he seeks to improve
personal and corporate stewardship not for his
own sake or security, but for the Christian witness and a more effective ministry.

The church's image and the preacher's influence are articulated in a letter from a government employee: "Society," he says, "has grown
so complex and cumbersome that the average
person is overwhelmed and has no confidence
in the ability of his institutions to solve problems.
. . . A minister must have the same basic attributes as leaders of other institutions." Plus, I
might add, sincere concern for the souls committed to his trust and their potential for the Lord's
kingdom. He must constantly attempt to dis-

cover and interpret God's agenda, and enlist people in its fulfillment. The pastor must be the most adroit and persistent of all administrators— he works with volunteers!

Successful companies and institutions have skilled employees, suave salesmen who specialize in promoting their employer's image and products. These "front runners" of good will are adept at pleasant and convincing rhetoric. They know the components of good advertising, the compensations of timing and exposure. They are called "PR" people.

Your minister is a publicist who is forever seeking to improve the image and ministry of the church he serves. Unlike the wizards of Madison Avenue and the commercial hucksters of radio and television, he, with perhaps the assistance of a few members, must create, mount, and promote whatever seems appropriate at "Old First" or "New Community Church." Generally speaking, there are two kinds of public relations with respect to the church: internal dissemination of information (i.e. promotion of ideas, programs, and goals within the congregation); and the external thrust to familiarize the community with the church's ministry.

There is also another dimension of church relations: it is known as cooperation. For example, the Protestant forces in your town decide to sponsor a Billy Graham Crusade. Your pastor may or may not be enamored with the idea. However, if he and his church do not participate, they are criticized and sometimes all but ostracized. Such an effort requires a tremendous amount of time and energy on the part of participating ministers. Regardless of additional work, his regular responsibilities run concurrently with the Crusade.

Some ministers are professional journalists who consistently publish articles and books. To others, writing can be painstakingly difficult, laborious, and time-consuming. Yet practically every pastor must assume some of the responsibilities of a writer. Modern congregations expect a weekly bulletin setting forth the order of worship, together with concerns of the parish. Whether it is a mimeographed sheet or an elaborate leaflet, the pastor's input is essential. Moreover, an increasing number of churches have parish papers that appear weekly or semimonthly. These publications usually require even more of the pastor's time and talent. In addition to writing a column, he must glean, edit, and see that material is produced and mailed on time.

Your minister will also write a variety of important letters during the week on behalf of his members, for friends searching for new employment, for ministers seeking relocation, and in support of worthy organizations soliciting funds.

ORNAMENT

Who wants to be ornamental at a public function? Your pastor is frequently asked to lend a profile of reverence and his "stained glass voice" in prayer for everything from the annual meeting of the Chamber of Commerce, luncheon groups, graduations and athletic banquets, to political rallies. Whatever one's interpretation of the appropriateness of prayer on such occasions, at the moment the pastor is not asked to be a reformer but a participant.

There are preachers who revel in public appearances. They like the sound of their voices; to see their names in print. Others loathe it. Whatever his personality and preference, your minister must be "Mr. Just Right" at more meetings than he would care to remember during the year.

COUNSELOR AND PASTOR

From the days when Jesus encountered distressed and diseased individuals until the present, devoted servants have made themselves available to the frustrated and needy. Nowadays we refer to these intimate conversations as counseling. The minister is supposed to be skilled in the art of listening, analyzing situations, detecting and voicing options. Many who come to your pastor are not his parishioners. In fact, I have discovered that, if the problems are serious and unduly embarrassing, troubled souls usually prefer to talk with a stranger.

If the preacher gains a reputation as a counselor, it can become very burdensome; or it can be a "cop-out" for lazy ministers. A denominational executive, when asked about the work habits of one of his pastors, demurred. After a thoughtful moment he replied, "Bill is a good man, but he spends too much time with other people's problems and not enough with his own members." Then he added this pensive comment: "The church can become a place to hide, you know, to avoid encounters with your parishioners."

This is not to speak disparagingly of the art of counseling—the ministry of sharing with and supporting frustrated human beings. Practition-

ers will testify to its tediousness and time consumption. A congregation may be unaware of
their pastor's involvement.

A couple was referred to me by an attorney.
After fifteen years of married life they were
starting separation procedures. While discussing
options with a lawyer, they were asked if they
would visit a clergyman. They agreed. He referred them to me. Since both were working,
appointments had to be at night and at a time
when few people, if any, would be using the
church buildings. They were sensitive to their
situation.

They arrived on time for our first conference,
a good sign. I tried to establish rapport and a
relaxed atmosphere. The wife had her arm in
a cast. When I asked if she had fallen, she said,
"No, my husband broke it." She was accused
of misappropriating their joint bank account and
running up bills in the city. He was charged
with being impersonal, critical, and incompati-
ble.

It was a tough case. Eventually we arrived
in our conversations to a point where confidence
and openness were displayed. At last we were
able to pray together; confessions were made;
love renewed. They professed their faith, were
baptized, and joined the Baptist Church! Yet
it had taken six long, grueling conferences on
my part. I do not regret this, and I am happy
if I influenced their decisions. I am simply re-
porting that counseling can be a time-consuming, enervating ministry.

"Louis XIV," declared Voltaire, "was not one
of the greatest men but certainly one of the
greatest kings that ever lived." It was said of

Edward VIII: "He was at his best only when the going was good." These comments should never describe a minister. There must be no contradiction between profession and performance. First, foremost, and always, he must be a decent, dependable, courageous Christian with spiritual stamina.

An able minister declared he would give his people a choice between having a preacher or a pastor as their leader. He said they could have his "head" or his "feet," but "they could not have both."

Controversy and comments continue. "He can preach, but he is a poor pastor." "He is a good pastor but a mediocre preacher." I suppose these two main functions of Christian ministry are indispensable and inseparable. Phillips Brooks claimed that, "The preacher, who is not a pastor, grows remote. The pastor, who is not a preacher, grows petty."

Unless the preacher knows people, his sermons have little sting against sin, and less compulsion to follow Christ. Part of his daily schedule includes counseling, marrying lovers, visiting members, blessing babies, calling on and praying for the sick and dying, burying the dead, comforting the sorrowing, encouraging the bewildered. Being a good pastor covers and includes a wide spectrum of ministries—all of which contribute to his understanding of people, as well as the direction and content for his preaching.

A good pastor will keep in touch with his people. In addition to normal midweek and Sunday responsibilities, the minister of a church of 150 souls located in a town of less than 5,000 citizens

reports he averages five programmatic meetings
a week, six community conferences, and ten pastoral calls.

The minister of a semisuburban parish of 325
members has three church meetings a week,
two community commitments, and makes
twenty-five pastoral calls.

A city pastor of 500 active members says he
averages seven church conferences per week,
three outside meetings, ten counseling sessions,
plus fifteen pastoral calls.

The senior minister of a metropolitan congregation of 2,000 souls averages three church
meetings a week, two community appearances,
four counseling sessions, twenty pastoral calls,
numerous staff conferences, twenty important
letters, not to mention innumerable telephone
calls.

Taking into account different communities,
program requirements, staff assistance, ap-
proaches, these samplings may suffice to indicate
the rather typical commitments of a pastor. The
Lord's work cannot be accomplished in a forty-
hour week!

EVANGELIST

The Gospels do not provide us with details
of Jesus' ministries. We are not familiar with his
methods of sermon preparation nor what constituted a pastoral call. Instead, we glimpse again
and again a profile of his purpose, how he became and continued to be Lord of Life. With
grace, consistency, and perseverance he moved
among people as if he were on a rescue mission,
which indeed he was. His teachings concerning

the lost are familiar, especially the parable of the lost sheep, the lost coin, and the lost son (Luke 15). The Great Commission (Matthew 28) admonishes believers to teach, preach, and baptize in his name.

Dwight L. Moody declared, "No man is really saved until he has won another." The quality of commitment constantly motivates the faithful pastor to seek out the lost, to challenge them to identify with Christ and his church.

The Medieval Church was wrecked by the spiritual deterioration of its leaders.

The minister must demonstrate impeccable Christian character. He cannot inspire his people to become what he is not, nor do what he refuses to attempt.

It is important that we remember and heed the counsel of the centuries, namely, the church is always within one generation of extinction! To avoid such a catastrophe, each generation of Christians has the obligation and privilege of presenting the gospel to all of God's children—near and far.

The average congregation must resist the temptation to operate a closed circuit show; of having a chubby club with a communion table and candlesticks to glorify its "nice" members, who have long since forgotten the haunting words of Jesus, "The Son of man came to seek and to save the lost" (Luke 19:10). "I am the way, and the truth, and the life; no one comes to the Father, but by me" (John 14:6).

In an indifferent, impersonal culture, programmed for early retirement and not eternal life, the minister struggles with the directive to seek the lost, within the church and the community. While the Great Commission was articulated by our Lord to lead to the Great Commitment, it is nonetheless the responsibility of the entire congregation to win souls to Christ.

The preacher must help develop a responsibility list; this would include the names of persons who need spiritual assistance, whom he feels should confess Christ and become active in the church. He must also recruit and train individuals to become concerned for and adept in reaching the lost. The effective minister is one who enables others to see what he sees, feel what he feels about Christ, and enlists them in the work of becoming persuasive evangelists.

PREACHER

Somewhere in this never-ending labyrinth the minister must find time to recuperate from day-to-day demands, to relax, renew his mind and spirit through meditation and prayer. Somewhere in his relentless schedule your pastor must find time for his family and his health.

However demanding the week, with its unanswered mail, disturbing telephone calls, radio or television scripts, inconsequential interruptions, denominational commitments, Sunday is approaching, and your minister must stand up to preach! He must have time to prepare his mind, spirit, and body. Although few if any will know of his frustrations and efforts during the turbulent week, the congregation expects him to look well, feel well, and preach well.

It was a great day for preaching when Bishop Gerald H. Kennedy of California, aged sixty, assumed the pastorate of First United Methodist Church, Pasadena. In acknowledging the call, this dynamic prelate said: "Ever since I became a bishop twenty years ago I have been homesick for a pulpit." This unorthodox, hard-hitting preacher reiterated his faith in the local church. "It seems to me that a bishop or any other bureaucrat needs to participate responsibly where the action is."

It is far easier to verbalize proclamations than to work with people; much safer to speak in an academic setting than in an exposed pulpit; less strenuous to administer denominational affairs than to assume the nitty-gritty problems of a congregation. The action has been and always will be in the local church!

To the average parishioner, what transpires in the sanctuary on Sunday morning is the sole criterion for the pastor's effectiveness and power. While this is unfair, I am afraid it is the prevailing attitude.

Your minister wants to preach well, but you must help him. See that he has adequate time to prepare. Periodically review his workload. Does he need assistance? Are there talented individuals in the congregation who could help him on a part-time volunteer or paid basis?

How many ministers have you worn out in your church? How many young people have you encouraged to enter the Christian ministry? Once I served a congregation that had been served by, altogether, eight ministers, but had not produced a single one! This is the kind of selfishness, ineptness, insensitivity that needs to be exposed. We always want someone else's son or daughter to proclaim the message, to make the sacrifice, to endure the continuing crucifixion.

Preaching is more than an attractive and persuasive arrangement of words. It is total life, commitment, and communication—proclaiming and practicing the Good News. It is passing around one's perforated heart for others to see and handle! Years of constant scrutiny and exposure take their toll, but it is still the most courageous and satisfying task in the world.

Don't underestimate your preacher!

If your minister is committed to Christ and devoted to the church—as I trust he is—he is constantly reviewing possible ways of communicating the wondrous love of Jesus. In different forms, nightly he prays after the manner of Another: "Lord, I have manifested your name to those whom you have entrusted to my ministry in Dallas, New York, Miami, Crooked Creek, and Fox Run. I have given them the words you gave me. I have served and loved them. Keep them forever in your love. . . ."

8
His Frustrations

Your preacher knows the meaning of Helmut Thielicke's phrase, "existential sickness." The conflict between what he should be and what he frequently must be is frustrating. If the modern minister could accomplish all that was expected of him, he would establish an endurance record for going without sleep.

If your pastor tries to protect himself from minutiae—as most people do—he risks the reputation of being a snob or an egotistical isolationist. If he does not, his study habits deteriorate to where his sermons are little more than a clever rearrangement of the headlines bounced off an appropriate Scripture. If any segment of society is justified in staging a protest, strike, or a march against the "Establishment," it is the clergy against the "good people" of the church who have allowed the ministry of Jesus Christ to become confused with, if not absorbed by, the myriad activities of the congregation!

Preachers are not crippled angels grounded for lack of pinion power, but vulnerable human

beings possessing all the passions, desires, and
needs of their parishioners. They, too, were once
whimpering babies. Some still are! Problems of
adolescence did not elude them. And domestic
dilemmas are common in the manse.

IDENTITY CRISIS

Your minister knows the thrust of Shake-
speare's haunting, penetrating question by King
Lear:"Who is it that can tell me who I am?"

Your pastor is forever asking himself, "Who
am I to be entrusted with the Good News of
Christ? Who am I to admonish people to follow
Jesus, to demonstrate his spirit, when I frequently sleep in contemporary gardens of Geth-
semane, and deny him in ways too numerous
to count?" The conscientious servant appreciates Paul's agony when he exclaimed, "I do not
understand my own actions. For I do not do
what I want, but I do the very thing I hate"
(Rom. 7:15).

His personality crisis carries over into professional identity. Unlike his peers, the minister
is variously addressed. He is called by many
names, not all of them complimentary. Saluta-
tions seem to vary with denominations, locale,
and attitudes.

Adherents to the Roman Catholic faith, for
instance, invariably refer to their spiritual leader
as "Father." The Jews address theirs as "Rabbi."
By nature, Protestantism invites, even nurtures,
diversity. If one has a doctorate, earned or con-
ferred, he may be so greeted and presented,
especially in formal settings.

The dubbing of "Preacher" is reminiscent of
frontier days, and, while an intimate designa-

tion, it is not altogether accurate, since it does not convey the scope of his responsibilities. The word "Pastor" is warm and relates easily to New Testament usage and is admiringly employed among some communions, especially Lutherans, with genuine affection. Yet the word has overtones of an agrarian era long since gone and with which few urbanites can meaningfully identify. The term "Reverend" should never be used without the article "the" preceding it and followed by "Mr." or "Dr." A correct introduction would be: "Please meet the Reverend Mr. Brown or the Reverend Dr. Smith." To address a minister as "Rev" is parochial and vulgar.

Added to his identity problem, parochial ambiguity, and misconceptions of the ministry, is the continuing debate among the so-called fathers of the church as to whose ministry is valid. This annoying concern is seldom exposed. Your pastor does not want to feel inferior to the religious hierarchy of the community, to be considered counterfeit, unacceptable. Does one have to be affiliated with an ecclesiastically structured bureaucracy, wear clericals, report to superiors, use liturgies and missals that are hundreds of years old to be in the authentic tradition of Christian priesthood? George Bernard Shaw's quip has strengthened and encouraged me at this point. "The only genuine apostolic succession would be in a cannibal tribe where the retiring witch doctor is consumed by his successors!"

Important as is official recognition, it is not exclusively the mystique of ordination that stamps one a minister of Christ; it is also his baptism, his growing Christian identity. The pulpit of such a proclaimer may be less ornate than in the great cathedrals, less remunerative than the pastor's salary in a burgeoning suburban parish, but who would discredit such a ministry?

Viewing emerging new ministries, Professor Richard Niebuhr used the term "pastoral director." Although fresh and in many ways an appealing designation, it nevertheless suggests a degree of separation in station and service which makes the expression objectionable to many.

During the frontier days of America and in some of the more orthodox communions and sects today, the word "Brother" is still associated with the spiritual leader. It is not only biblical but intimate and suggestive of a relationship mutually shared and appreciated.

Visualizing the minister as an enabler, an equipper, the word "Coach" has been suggested to describe the spiritual head of a congregation. Although there are interesting parallels between an athletic coach and a minister, the appellation is inadequate. The coach knows his players better than they know themselves; to teach them requires more time and patience than to participate in the game itself. An important role of any coach is to encourage and support his players, having the perception to see their potential and the psychological insights to motivate and develop them. Many become "father confessors" to their players. The coach sends them out to implement his instructions, and he does not hesitate to "yank" them when they make a mistake, though the eyes of fifty thousand spectators may be upon them.

A minister's role is more nearly that of a shop superintendent or foreman who has two principal functions: training workers in desired skills necessary to achieve given objectives, and seeing that they produce. The preacher is commissioned to prepare individuals to bear fruit, to work in the Lord's vineyards. He must observe their ministries and encourage them. As much as he would like to make changes, he dare not yank a lazy elder or a poor teacher; unlike the shop foreman, he cannot fire or penalize an unproductive committeeman.

Since a minister is evaluated, respected, and loved not according to titles but by performance, to observe him may suggest the most affectionate and accurate greeting. You may feel so close to him that you want to use the word "Father" or "Brother" or even his first name, as many prefer. In any event, do not call your pastor anything behind his back that you would not say to his face. It would be courteous to ask him how he prefers to be addressed.

TITLES SELDOM TELL

Ministers frequently frustrate their colleagues by attitude and action. This baffles the laity! We had gathered in the elegant study of a cathedral-like church situated on one of the most famous boulevards in America. The occasion was to celebrate the founding of our country in a union service of Thanksgiving. Overawed by giants of the pulpit as they robed and joked with one another, I, a lowly associate, donned the robe suggested by the senior minister—the only one left! The gown bore on its sleeves chevrons indicating the wearer possessed a doctorate. When a prominent pulpiteer saw me in the gown, he looked disapprovingly down his nose—his glasses precariously near the end of it—and growled, "That's a doctor's robe. You can't wear it. . . ."

What a cutting comment! I was saved from
utter embarrassment by the quick perception
of the host pastor, who jokingly said to the self-
appointed guardian of chancel vestments and
colors, ". . . he will soon have a doctorate. Don't
you think it would be all right for him to get
used to its weight?"

Laughter followed!

It was a beautiful and moving service. However, that preacher's sermon was plastic and
pompous, because he had placed himself on a
pedestal. By attitude and utterance he had mo-
mentarily destroyed a young pastor's sense of
personhood. Preachers can be arrogant and obnoxious.

Reflecting on the bigot's reprimand, I tried
to visualize Jesus sending out the Twelve, later
the Seventy, to share their faith and love but
first deputizing husky Simon Peter to make certain their robes reflected their spiritual stations,
that they entered the villages and homes of
those whom they sought to convert according
to rank and stature. Instead, the Lord said, "Behold, I send you out as lambs in the midst of
wolves. Carry no purse, no bag, no sandals; and
salute no one on the road. Whatever house you
enter, first say, 'Peace be to this house!' " (Luke
10:3–5).

Irrespective of the source, it is frustrating to
discover individuals in the church who place
station above service, façade above faithfulness.

DOUBLE STANDARDS

Preachers are frequently perplexed by double
standards practiced by parishioners in areas of
economic, social, and moral conduct. The life

styles of members are often in stark contrast to those endured by their pastors. Nowhere is the distinction clearer than in how they earn and spend their money. Many parishioners look askance at a minister with business expertise; they are suspicious and sometimes suggest his salary be frozen or decreased because of additional income. Members do not live by the same rules. They dabble in all kinds of businesses and make deals for profit.

Here is a deacon, with an excellent income, who periodically takes his pastor and wife to the country club for dinner and political exposure, a plush place where the annual dues are twice the amount he gives his church. All during dinner he complains about the church's budget escalating when general liquidity is uncertain.

An elder, conservative but generous and kind, felt his pastor should never play cards or take "a drink." One night we called unannounced. From the windows we could see a card party in progress. As would be expected, there was a swift and hilarious rearrangement of the room before answering the door. This type of hypocrisy the pastor rightfully resents.

Such conduct causes the preacher to realize that few know who he is. They forget his humanity, isolate him, perpetuate dual standards and deception.

INFLEXIBILITY

A congregation's allergy to change is exceedingly difficult for any pastor. In his book, *Sunday, A Minister's Story,* John C. Harper, rector of St. John's Church, Washington, D.C., shares a humorous yet provocative comment from a friend when he first moved to the nation's capital. " 'John, you can preach heresy there, you can even be immoral if you want to, but for heaven's sake, don't move the candles on the altar!' "

What was said in jest is so hauntingly true that it ceases to be funny. Every congregation has its "untouchable" candlesticks, unwritten laws, unannounced expectations.

These holy articles and objects of faith are sometimes indicated by the version of Scripture used in worship, attire of the minister, the disciplines practiced, and the pronouncements uttered.

Less visible than tampering with the arrangement of the chancel, or the color of the walls, or the carpet in the sanctuary are such forbidden altars as what kind of musical instrument is used, or church school literature studied, or the time of the annual revival. It is tantamount to expulsion for any clergyman or layman to tamper with parochial lock boxes of beliefs!

However biblical the orientation of one's faith, if it is isolated from issues of society, from the problems and concerns of people, then corporate worship is little more than a religious huddle on Sunday, an indefensible presumption.

It is so easy for an institution, especially a church, to lock itself into cozy little rituals and regulations, slavishly following precast procedures and services, that it can easily separate itself from the growing edges of spiritual renewal and ministry.

Historic congregations must struggle to avoid becoming museums; newer ones must strive to rise above temptations of self-pity while sacrificing for facilities.

Resistance to change—inflexibility—is a common sin of every church.

Irrespective of denominational posture, the Church of Jesus Christ must be a redemptive, not a restricted, fellowship; a confessing, forgiving, and serving community, not the religious equivalent of secular success.

The church is the Lord's movable feast!

Dr. Ralph W. Neighbour, Jr., was well aware of candlestick parishioners when he wrote *The Seven Last Words of The Church.* More accurately stated they are: "We never did it that way before!"

POLITICS OF POWER

Ministers are frequently victims of politics in the parish. Practically every congregation has a few influential people who can either cause or prevent significant actions. To have a clique running a church unofficially is disgusting, but to have families who have money calling the shots surreptitiously is not only devastating to the democratic process, but makes it impossible for the pastor to mount and service a program. Poor rich people can wreck a church and destroy ministers.

INERTIA

Few if any problems in a parish are more frustrating than inertia, the lassitude of people. The pastor realizes what needs to be done, for he has been trained in analyzing church situations. He has the expertise and energy to accomplish needed ministries, but there is inadequate interest and response. Nothing is more exasperating

to your minister! Unlike a well-calibrated businessman, he is for the most part working with
volunteers. He cannot make demands, only suggestions. Then he must use the power of example.

He spends much time orienting new members
to places of responsibility, many of whom have
neither the background nor personality to comprehend or fulfil assignments. He does not have
the power to replace a person who is not fulfilling his ministry. Flattering and cajoling, he tries
every known psychological approach to motivate response. But there is precious little he can
do, except wait until the annual meeting and
the selection of new committees, hoping for better informed and more energetic workers.

If not audibly, your pastor frequently quotes
to himself words directed to the early Asian
churches, especially the warning to the brethren
at Laodicea: " 'I know your works: you are neither cold nor hot. Would that you were cold
or hot! So, because you are lukewarm, and neither cold nor hot, I will spew you out of my
mouth' " (Rev. 3:15,16).

I am troubled over the general attitude of
many laymen toward the ministry and the attitude of many ministers toward the church. I
would not be so presumptuous as to prescribe
a cure-all for the muddle in which we find ourselves, but certainly it would be helpful for
schools and seminaries to work more closely
with churches in the selection and training of
preachers. Divinity schools dare not isolate
themselves from the real world; the church has
no right to dictate the curriculum and faculty.
But there should be open and continuing communication between and from all sectors of the

Christian community regarding the preparation and performance of its servants if frustration is to be minimized.

As we review some of the irritations and attitudes that "bug" ministers, it is hoped that you may help free your pastor from parish claustrophobia and frustration.

Clergy resent Sunday sourness: the sad face, white shirt, black tie, beardless concept of leadership. A member of a pulpit committee with whom I was conferring immediately registered her negative reaction to a candidate under consideration for their pulpit because, according to the photograph, he wore a beard. She had never met the man nor heard him preach, but he did not fit her stereotype of what a preacher should look like.

Ministers are tired of being referred to, directed, and treated as "hired" personnel. There is a responsibility here, and every conscientious pastor recognizes it and strives to be worthy of his employment. But, as we have said, he is not paid to keep up an institution; rather, he is compensated that he may experience freedom to preach. You can no more pay your minister for a meaningful sermon, a crucial hospital call, a baptismal, a wedding, or a funeral service than you can adequately pay a doctor for delivering your baby or a surgeon for saving your life. There are some things money cannot buy; caring is one of them.

As a group, preachers are among the most generous and consistent stewards in the Christian community. The majority are proportionate givers, many exceeding the biblical tithe. It is, therefore, disturbing to have prominent members of a congregation making decisive financial decisions, when their stewardship is anything but commendable. This is hard to take!

Ministers are weary of having to fight for every inch of progress made in the local church and tired, too, of having to explain the irresponsibility of professing Christians whose conduct disturbs the community.

Pastors are fed up with denominational bureaucrats and community boosters who use them and refer to them as "key persons" in obtaining desired objectives. Your minister is considered by many as a mysterious locksmith, endowed with special gifts for opening closed doors. Those who flatter and exploit your pastor frequently reduce him to little more than the honorary key awarded by the mayor of your city to a celebrity. It photographs beautifully and warrants applause at the banquet, but, in reality, it opens no doors!

Ministers are weary of committee meetings; weary of carpings by members who have dull axes to grind, prejudices to peddle, scores to settle; weary of listening to "the minutes of the last meeting" where trivia was discussed in astonishing detail and precious hours wasted.

Lazy laity who talk an ambitious church program and then expect their minister to implement it are a headache. Nothing is more frustrating to your pastor than living with inertia, doing your work and his, too. Ministers are weary of their workloads but not weary in the Lord's work.

Good ambassadors of Christ are tired of popular criticism and parish problems—indeed embarrassed by them—but they are not tired of the ministry. Your pastor is called to serve, not to succeed by the criteria of the Chamber of Commerce.

Despite harassments and disappointments, most ministers love their work and are faithful in their responsibilities. The chancellor of a fine university once invited me to become chaplain of his academic community. It was an attractive setting. I was strongly tempted to identify with the institution. However, after wrestling with the decision, among other reasons I cited in my declination, "Life would not be the same without the frustrations of the parish!"

9
His Support

In this chapter we consider not the financial support but a wide spectrum of thoughtful acts and concerns which buttress the pastor's pride and spirit.

Being fallible human beings, ministers are often discouraged and disillusioned by life's inequities, the conduct of church members and leaders in high places. Pastors need smiles and reassurances. Like Cleopas, trudging toward Emmaus after the Lord's crucifixion, the road home can be painful and lonely. These are highly vulnerable moments. The subtleties of Satan are tempting; words of the Savior seem distant and irrelevant.

Life's encounters test resiliency and faith. Your pastor lives with unique and merciless pressures. Church people can be both tedious and troublesome. Knowing that some individuals will disturb, if not destroy a meeting; knowing that certain members are in disagreement with your pastor—and are out to embarrass him—let the preacher know you are with him in the struggle to Christianize your church and community! Perhaps an added greeting after the meeting, more strength in the handclasp, a thoughtful telephone call, a letter, or a thank-you note—all can be indications of supportiveness.

ENCOURAGEMENT

While preparing these paragraphs, I was prompted to rummage through two sizable files of letters from former parishioners. Here are the opening sentences of a long, handwritten letter from a woman in her seventies, whose remarkable son, president of our congregation, died suddenly. Some of us felt he had given his life for his church.

How shall I begin this note!

First, I wish to personally thank you, which sounds so inadequate, for the wonderful Christian memorial service for my precious son. . . . My heart ached for you, and I realized, more than ever before, the heartaches of our ministers in their shepherding of their flocks. I am praying for you that someone will be found to take up in the service of our church as willingly and optimistically as
. . . .

His was one of the most difficult funerals I ever conducted. I have had the usual number of deaths to face plus suicides and as many as seven from one family killed in an automobile accident. But this was the only memorial service where I literally wept.

During an unusually hectic fall, a busy insurance executive wrote:

> In the midst of this Advent Season, may I take this means to thank you for your constancy of effort in our joint work at the church.

After an unfortunate misunderstanding by a well-to-do woman who misinterpreted what I had said, she later apologized:

> Where have you left a deeper impression than on the lives and in the hearts of your own flock, to whom you have given yourself so unstintingly in service and loving deeds, and you and yours are loved more deeply by everyone than any pastor I remember . . . . I wish we expressed our appreciation more often.

On a low Monday I received this word of encouragement from an unexpected source:

> I feel I must tell you what a powerful and effective sermon I think you preached yesterday. The theme of cheating, in its expanded interpretation, could apply to everyone, yet was so fine for the students present.

Following an emotional outburst from one of the officers of the church during a meeting that was very unsettling, a banker wrote:

> The subject of . . . remarks at the close of our general board meeting Sunday night was not only astonishing, but disillusioning and disappointing. How any member of our congregation could have been so thoughtless and inconsiderate is completely beyond my comprehension. . . . Ours is

a great church, and we concur in your thinking that it has a tremendous future. May I just add that all three of us are with you 100%.

Such comments sharpen the preacher's courage, keep him strong and ready to serve.

ATTITUDE

Attitude is important to your minister. Like a traffic light, it flashes "caution," "go," or "stop." It is not always necessary to concur in what your pastor proposes, but your response, demeanor, language, and general attitude endear or separate you from the fellowship. An optimistic, fairminded Christian response not only generates respect, but contributes to the authenticity of the congregation's search for community. Discipleship is not synonymous with self-will.

Attitudes inevitably determine victory or defeat, progress or fragmentation. And nowhere is this phenomenon more apparent than in the church.

In his autobiography, *The Living of These Days,* Harry Emerson Fosdick declared that no pastor was ever surrounded by abler and more dedicated men and women than he had at Riverside Church. Dr. Fosdick said that Mr. John D. Rockefeller, Jr., was one of "the most considerate, friendly, self-effacing, cooperative persons" he had ever known. The beloved pastor reported that he had seen Mr. Rockefeller, as a trustee, argue against a certain proposal. But when outvoted, he would accept the chairmanship of the committee to implement the program he had previously disapproved.

This, I submit, is churchmanship! Such discipleship is contagious. Members with such vision and spirit are not far from the kingdom of God; the church is close to her Lord.

ATTENDANCE

Attendance at any gathering speaks volumes. Attendance at worship, fellowship occasions, and work sessions is a visible expression of support and belief.

She was almost ninety years old. Her locomotion was poor; the dear soul could not see well; her hearing was impaired. Yet she managed to attend worship virtually every Sunday. Although her family was patient and extremely attentive, her faithful attendance nevertheless required considerable effort on the part of this sweet octogenarian.

After worship one day I overheard a cluster of active women talking to the little lady. One congratulated her on being at church. Another complimented her "just right" attire. Still another commented, "Mrs. . . . , you say you don't see or hear well and that it's painful to walk. I hope you're not overdoing by coming to worship."

Obviously annoyed, the gallant soul quipped, "Don't you think my presence counts for anything?"

Indeed! To see this courageous soul sitting two pews from the pulpit was not only an inspiration to the pastor but to all who knew her.

Too many professing Christians have the strange notion that church attendance is nice, rewarding at times, but not necessary to Christian growth and ministry. We are not recommending attendance awards! It has taken the church a long time to recover—if it has—from the numbers racket so many congregations played to the rhythm of "Onward Christian Soldiers."

However, there is a positive and substantive side to church attendance. It is a visible means of supporting the gospel. It is a witness! There is therapy and power in numbers, especially when the group has assembled with the common objective of confessing their sins, acknowledging their needs, and recommitting themselves to the merciful Father. Attendance is an acknowledgment of spiritual renewal, a willingness to assume new ministries.

Fraternities, sororities, civic organizations, professional and business groups, athletic clubs and teams stress the importance of fulfilling one's duty and the privilege of being present for specific occasions. Fines are frequently levied against absentees. Membership in most organizations is contingent upon one's presence and participation. Not so in the church! We coddle the indifferent, inactive members. "No shows" trouble owners of professional athletic teams. It is a bad omen, but it is normal in most churches.

This was clearly echoed while I was working with a congregation on a new constitution and by-laws. When it came to establishing quorums for conducting business, following suggestions from its denominational penthouse—it was agreed that 25 percent of the members of its board would constitute a legal meeting and 40 percent of the congregation. Are our expectations too low?

Nothing is more encouraging to your pastor than your presence at stated services of worship, fellowship, and committee meetings. Attendance is a vote of confidence. It is also an indication that persons are searching for grace, reaching out for Christian fellowship. Absenteeism is too ambivalent to assess. It certainly breeds indifference and suspicion. Whatever may be wrong in your church, staying away will not correct it.

It should not be forgotten that Pentecost occurred—the emergence of the Church with irresistible power—not in a half-filled sanctuary, but in obedient hearts filled with hope (Acts 2:1–4). In response to the Lord's directive to tarry in Jerusalem, the frightened but trusting souls assembled. Suddenly there was the rush of a mighty wind, and the Holy Spirit found, cleansed, and inspired the 120 souls who waited as they had been commanded. They were together in expectancy and faith! Spiritual power awaits the congregation that fulfills the conditions of Pentecost.

Regular sincere church attendance generates enthusiasm, creates an atmosphere conducive to the visitation of the Spirit, fuses a congregation together in oneness and ministry. Miracles are not limited to Christ's church, but they continue to occur. Like early believers, faithful worshipers are renewed in body, mind, and spirit.

You can make up—as it were—your attendance at a luncheon group, but it is impossible to recapture the transforming power of public worship. That is why, however technically correct and beautifully transcribed a service may be reproduced, the warmth, magnetism, and miraculous qualities of human personality commingling in song, prayer, listening to the Word read and interpreted, participating in symbolic observances, cannot be duplicated. They must be experienced. Spiritual togetherness is nontransferable!

JOYOUS PARTICIPATION

"I have said this to you, that in me you may have peace. In the world you have tribulation; but be of good cheer, I have overcome the world" (John 16:33). The sheer valor and beauty of these words of Jesus directed to his disciples toward the close of his earthly ministry reduced Thomas Carlyle to tears. Our Lord spoke not out of isolation, but fresh from the arena of conflict and suffering, anticipation and trust. He had experienced disappointment, hypocrisy, and embarrassment. Time was running out, hope dwindling. Yet, as he stood on the rubble of his shattered dreams, he exclaimed, "Be of good cheer, I have overcome the world."

If we really believed Jesus had overcome the world and we were recipients of his grace and kingdom, our disciplines and devotion would be more genuine, our participation in his work more cheerful.

Quintus Septimius Florens Tertullian, a third-century Roman theologian, said, "The Christian saint is hilarious." What a delightful comment! We think of a joke, a miscue by a public performer, as being hilarious, but we don't feel the same way about a Christian. This is partly true because, for too long, followers of Christ have assumed the stance of sadness. Most members of the church are as melancholy as a loser at Las Vegas.

Jesus was a joyous person. He had a sense of
humor. Think of an old self-righteous Pharisee
carefully straining out a gnat from his soup because it was unclean and then figuratively swal-
lowing a camel! In their punctiliousness to avoid
tiny particles of defilement, they consumed
larger doses.

Ecological prerequisites are constantly articulated. Daily we are admonished to clean up and
protect our environment. Clean air is essential
to good health, and so is the spiritual air we
breathe. If we persist in living with complaints,
fault-finding, and moodiness, we destroy relationships and our own well-being. It is reported
that Matthew Arnold had a weakness for com-
plaining. When he died a neighbor quipped,
"Poor Matthew, he won't like God!"

Living with an increasing awareness of God's
world and his expectations enhances and increases joy and spiritual vitality.

Joy is not the absence of pain or perplexity.
It is not synonymous with pleasure. Pleasure is
usually associated with physical and mental activity. Joy is the flowering of the spirit! It is an
achievement, a sense of fulfillment. It cannot
be bequeathed; it must be acquired. It is a quality of life, not a quantity of possessions.

Joy is essentially social. It cannot be isolated.
There is an unmistakable contagion about a joyous person. After observing Phillips Brooks, the
great preacher, a Boston reporter said, "It
was a dull, rainy day when things looked dark
and lowering, but Phillips Brooks came down
through newspaper row, and all was bright."
There was sunshine, gladness, joy, and friendliness in the face of the beloved bishop which
was a benediction to all.

Bring joy and thanksgiving with you to church, whether to a committee meeting, conference with the pastor, or public worship. You will be blessed, and you will be a blessing to others. Participate cheerfully.

MEANINGFUL GIFTS

Dr. William Barclay, distinguished preacher, author, and long-time member of the Divinity Faculty of the University of Glasgow, lost his mother to cancer in 1932, the same year he was licensed to preach. He was obsessed by the question: "Why should my mother, lovely in body and in spirit, good all through, have to die like that?"

His father assured him he would have a new dimension in his preaching. Barclay later wrote:

> The last thing she ever gave me was a soft leather sermon case—and from that day to this, more than forty years later, I never went into a pulpit without it. I thank God on every remembrance of my mother.

Personal gifts can be a source of continuing encouragement.

A most unusual man, not a member of our congregation, worshiped with us frequently. He gave the church a sizeable sum of money for its ministers' continuing education, books, and travel. This prominent industrialist, son of a minister, remembering how hard-pressed his father had been financially most of his life, desired to assist pastors in their search for truth, to afford them opportunities denied his father. He admired the high calling; this was his way of encouraging preachers.

ENTERTAINMENT

Entertainment can be relaxing and rewarding. Everyone needs a change of pace and schedule, to meet different people, be exposed to new concerns and settings. This is particularly true of the pastor, whose responsibilities are demanding and tend to be restrictive.

Perceptive churchmen will entertain their minister and his family not out of a sense of duty or so frequently as to be burdensome, but as a means of getting to know the family and surrounding them with friendship and love. Entertaining, if not carefully planned, can be hectic for all concerned. Spur-of-the-moment invitations are sometimes exciting and fulfilling, but not as a regular practice. Besides, what if all parishioners followed a similar impulse?

Where possible, call and suggest dates for an evening in the home, restaurant, or club. A pastor is like an athlete living with pregame jitters. Friday and Saturday evenings are usually occupied, and Sunday is too overwhelming to be relaxing. Except in rare instances try to respect the preacher's disciplines. Suggest a time that will provide maximum freedom. Tell him in advance your plans for the evening so that he can make suitable adjustments and dress appropriately.

When entertained in your home, the pastor appreciates being included in the normal procedures and prayer patterns of the family. Although he will, of course, offer the blessing if asked, he would much prefer for the father, mother, or child to thank God for the occasion and the food. Moreover, the table prayer is a good time to audibly express gratitude for your association with the pastor, his family, and your church. It can and should be more than a repeated table thanksgiving. Explore pleasant areas of conversation. Make your guests feel at home.

It is not possible for every member of the congregation to entertain the preacher's family, particularly in a large parish. Nor does everyone have adequate living and dining space, not to mention budget requirements. Some of the loveliest parties we recall are those that were cohosted by two or three families at a favorite restaurant or club.

Speaking of clubs, you may want your minister to enjoy membership in a good club where he and his family can entertain or slip away once in awhile. When we were in St. Louis, some of the members felt I should belong to the Missouri Athletic Club. Although one of my sponsors was on the board of directors, it required a considerable waiting period. This rather expensive membership provided our family with many happy hours. Moreover, it afforded opportunities to minister, to attract individuals to our church who otherwise would not have been contacted. This elegant old club was an ideal place to meet for lunch, dinner, or to entertain guests.

Some churches need to learn the compensations of beauty and serenity. There are congregations that are so aware of costs—not because they are financially insolvent, but because of their meager concept of the ministry—that they compel their pastors to be miserly. Little wonder some people gain the impression churches are inferior institutions without expense accounts. Prudence has its place, but love is a spendthrift! He who represents the best should be at home with the best.

My first job out of seminary was that of Field and Alumni Secretary for my alma mater, Lynchburg College, Lynchburg, Virginia. It was during the thirties, when money was scarce, but people were proud and, for the most part, honorable. Yet, in this depression period, the president of the college instructed me, when on the road, to stay in the best hotels and motels. "The higher price," he said, "is worth the difference. I want you to be proud of the institution you represent and the people with whom you associate and communicate."

What have you done lately, in a social or economic way, to make your minister proud of being pastor of your church?

RECREATION

Historically, ministers have had the reputation of being lazy and obese, good eaters and poor performers, anything but the epitome of Paul's declaration: "Do you not know that you are God's temple and that God's Spirit dwells in you?" (1 Cor. 3:16).

It is difficult for a soft specimen of humanity to sparkle with the Spirit. Many Americans grow flabby because of their unwillingness to exercise in proportion to their food consumption. When asked what he did for exercise, Chauncey Mitchell Depew replied, "I get my exercise serving as pallbearer to my friends who exercise."

Your minister attends his share of funerals, but it requires more than participation in professional responsibilities to keep one mentally and physically fit. Everyone must go beyond the rigors of his day if he would know the exhilaration of genuine wellness.

Rest and relaxation are as necessary for the minister as for any other combat soldier. He needs to separate himself from schedule and deadlines to review his mission, to read and contemplate objectives for the ensuing year. Moreover, the preacher welcomes the opportunity to explore common interests with the family, become better acquainted, renew solidarity and faith. A well-planned vacation can be a profitable investment for both parishioners and pastor.

At a time when bodily fitness is obviously poor, encourage your pastor to keep physically fit. A Christian has been described as a spiritual athlete in the pink of condition! Recreation and exercise will not only enhance your pastor's appearance and increase his stamina, but they will also sharpen his mind. If he has been a competitive athlete, he may be inclined to spend too much time in the local gymnasium or on the golf course. The opposite, however, is frequently true: namely, former athletes sometimes turn away from exercise altogether.

If your spiritual shepherd has little interest in physical activity, find out what is available in the community and what appeals to him. Encourage him to participate in a regular activity so that he will not nurse a guilt complex while hiking, sailing, bicycling, or whatever. It came as a welcome surprise to me in a small church to have one of its members provide me with membership in a health club. I could have afforded it, but he wanted to do this for his pastor. I was grateful not only for his generosity, but also that he recognized the benefits afforded by such an institution. Eventually I worked out a routine requiring less than an hour five days a week. It became a part of my daily schedule—a remunerative investment.

The athletic director of a prominent university once told me, "As we grow older, we do not need more exercise; we need to exercise more."

BE A VOLUNTEER

During the development of this book, the minister of one of the largest churches in Methodism wrote: "It takes more and more effort to get the same results. On the other hand," he continued, "the most satisfying encounters are to see people come alive through the fellowship in the church."

Getting members to accept responsibility is every pastor's problem. What a joy to have intelligent, consecrated parishioners volunteer for difficult ministries which require preparation and constant perseverance.

How well I remember a board meeting in a certain metropolitan parish. Concern was voiced that we were not reaching a sufficient number of persons for Christ. We were in general agreement as to what should be done, but no one was willing to commit himself to the task. There were searching moments of silence. Then, quite unexpectedly, a prominent physician stood and said, "I don't know much about evangelism, but I love Christ and his church. Pastor, if you will teach me how to become an evangelist and if you, the members of this board, will cooperate, I will head up our evangelism program for next year."

It was an exciting statement! Like a transfusion, he injected new life and enthusiasm into the group. We experienced a great ingathering of souls that year. Moreover, the physician grew in Christian grace and loyalty, as did the congregation.

READ, RENEW, RELATE

From Paul's admonition to be transformed "by the renewal of your mind" (Rom. 12:2), to modern stimuli to read, Christians are challenged to be informed. Ignorance and indifference are twin tyrants, constantly obstructing spiritual progress.

The Reverend Nelson Price, director of the Division of Public Media for the United Methodist Church Communication, said at Randolph-Macon College, Ashland, Virginia, in 1977 that other than working hours, viewing television is "the most prevalent activity of the average American." Annually, a typical citizen spends 1200 hours watching television, 200 hours reading newspapers, 200 hours reading magazines, and ten hours reading books! Mr. Average American works 2,000 hours a year.

In such an atmosphere, it is exceedingly difficult to discipline oneself to read—to be informed about the world and nation, the relevancy and imperativeness of the gospel in a managed society.

Exceptional individuals have been and are prodigious readers: Adolf Hitler, Winston Churchill, and Thomas Wolfe all claimed to have devoured thousands of books. Dr. Karl Menninger, eminent psychiatrist, at age 84 reads 20 to 30 books a month.

To some people reading is a pleasure; to others it is hard work. Some read two or three books concurrently. Others seldom read at all. Books are people!

If one is what he reads—or fails to read—and he *is* very largely, then many church members are mere statistics.

But you say, "I do not have time to read." Few persons have the luxury of uninterrupted reading hours. One must learn to utilize the tag ends of time. It is amazing how much one can learn in segments of 10, 20, or 40 minutes a day. The median reading speed is estimated to be from 295 to 325 words per minute. Accepting this as a reasonable norm and that average books run 40,000 to 50,000 words, then a normal reader could cover a book in two and a half to three and a half hours. Many can read a book in an hour! How do you read? What do you read outside of your professional and trade journals? Do you read the Bible and the periodicals of your church? Do you read books with a religious message?

Reading is a marvelous experience. The one who reads the most lives the most. He who reads intelligently has by far the best chance to live helpfully. To read Christian literature is to enhance one's effective witness.

Knowing of my interest in literature, my lay friends have given me exciting input from time to time. Their ideas have triggered articles, sermons, and books. Read and help your pastor communicate the gospel.

PRAYER

One of the moving moments in my life was leading a prayer service for the Minister Ecu-

menical of our congregation. Following a period
of poor health and coaxing, the scholarly saint
agreed to go into the hospital. Tests revealed
he needed surgery. There was justifiable concern; he was an old man. With characteristic
courage he elected to have the operation.

The day before surgery I ministered to him.
It was an inspiring experience. His magnani-
mous spirit did more for me than I did for him.
Knowing he was closely identified with the men
of the congregation, I was prompted to say, "Tomorrow when you go to surgery, we'll be praying for you in the sanctuary." My statement
brought tears to his eyes and prompted the comment: "Thank you. That would be nice. . . ."

A few telephone calls were made.

Next morning, despite short notice and down-
town traffic, at eight o'clock about sixty business-
men filed into the sanctuary to participate in
a provocative service of music, scripture, and
prayers. It was a spiritual summit. Not one of
us could ever be the same.

A year or so later, when this lyrical preacher
had recovered and concluded a powerful message to a large gathering of his brethren, a denominational leader was heard to say, "Who
knows but what that prayer meeting, held in
his behalf, preserved him for this hour?"

Do not forget to pray for your pastor. You
expect him to pray for you and your loved ones.
But do you methodically and earnestly ask God
to bless and direct him? It could make a difference in your relationship. Your pastor does not
have a pastor!

A congregation we once served decided to
upgrade its minister by sending him on a world
tour. It was a generous and concrete expression

of love. Preparations were carefully made, including the underwriting of a sizeable insurance policy payable to my family in case of accident or death.

On the eve of my departure I was invited to the chapel. Without my knowledge officers of the church had invited representatives from the various sectors and organizations within the congregation. The president presided over the worship, in which several participated. Among other personalizations was the spreading of my itinerary on the altar. The leader articulated concern, joy, and constant prayer for me while away. Furthermore, I was assured they would do whatever was needed for the family in my absence. We shared the Lord's Supper together. It was a foretaste of heaven! In the lonely weeks and months to come the fellowship of that hour was a movable and sustaining feast.

How long has it been since you surprised your pastor with a prayer service to honor and undergird him?

I have always been a prodigious dreamer. For better or worse, two or three times a week I am involved in exhaustive, fanciful adventures. Many are so vivid and dramatic that I awaken with a start and find it difficult to go back to sleep. At other times I have been able to resume a dream once interrupted. Sometimes these night thoughts deal with past activities, a replay, as it were, of life's high moments, ranging from sporting events to spiritual ecstasy.

A year or so ago I had a remarkable dream; I was on a world preaching mission. After participating in a variety of worship settings, including military installations, I returned home via aircraft carrier. The "flat-top" was attractively arranged for the occasion. Despite worsening weather, a large crowd of air personnel and seamen assembled. During the gathering storm, winds increased; the mighty ship began to roll as unbelievable waves lashed her decks. Some sailors were all but swept into the sea. As a frightening gust of wind and cascading walls of water enveloped us, a huge and kindly sailor unexpectedly threw his arms around me, saying, "Preach on, brother; I've got you!"

Without retrospective analysis, this nightdream has become a daydream, constantly reminding me that God's Word will not return empty, but will accomplish what he desires (Isa. 55:11). Support frequently comes from unexpected places.

The faithful preacher and his parishioners are assured of visible and invisible support. Here it is: "The eternal God is your dwelling place, and underneath are the everlasting arms" (Deut. 33:27).

10
His Love

Whether you know it or not, your minister loves you. He may not approve of some of your ideas or actions. Your attitude may irritate him, and your stewardship may perplex him. Even so, he is your best friend. He will come to your aid whether you are the president of the congregation or a delinquent member, honored by the community or sentenced by a court of justice; in bankruptcy or affluence—your pastor attempts to leave deposits of love. Like leaven in dough, his spirit penetrates and empowers persons to rise to higher levels of reality and response.

The power of the pastor's presence was dramatically confirmed in an experience a few years ago. A parishioner, president of a bank, had gone through the harrowing experience of having his wife disappear. Days, weeks, months stretched into years. At last she was pronounced legally dead.

Eventually my friend remarried.

Then one day, as if parachuting from the skies,

she reappeared! The city croaked with gossip.
Newspapers headlined the story. Pictures, quotations, and speculations constituted a cruel replay. I had to visit her former husband. I had
no idea of his reaction to the publicity or to
my presence. It would be a delicate encounter.
Standing in the foyer of the bank—in full view
of his office—I asked God to direct me and my
troubled friend. No sooner had I finished than
the financier glimpsed me through the door and
called, "Come in, preacher!"

I approached with a smile and outstretched
hand. Politely he stood and grasped my hand
with a firm clasp. His eyes watered. We did not
sit down. With all the calmness and affection
at my command, addressing him by his first
name, I said, "God bless you. I bring you greet-
ings from our church. We believe in you, and
we love you." That was all I said, but it was
enough. Gracefully he carried on his professional, personal, and church responsibilities.

Months later, having accepted an invitation
to serve a metropolitan congregation in a distant
city, I received a telephone call from a prominent tailor. He was calling for an appointment
to measure me for a suit. I assured him I had
not engaged his firm's services. "A friend is giving you a suit," he replied.

"Can this friend afford it?"

"Yes, indeed."

You guessed it! The banker sent the tailor to
my study with instructions: "I want him to have
your best." It was the finest suit I have ever
had. When later I thanked him in a note and
verbally, he replied with characteristic candor,
"Preacher, if you must go, I want you to go first
class!"

Do you love your pastor as you do your physician?

In some moment of stress you may have shared the Hindu poet-philosopher Rabindranath Tagore's observation, "When you took your leave I found God's footprints on my floor." This beautiful thought should symbolize, and frequently does so, the earnest pastor when he takes his leave from a home, hospital, or office. It might conclude a conversation at the post office, on the street corner, at the gasoline station, or with the elevator operator. Patrol boys protecting their peers at an intersection know him. Strangers and those who will never come to hear him preach will be challenged by his kindness, encouraged by his friendliness, comforted by his words.

MATURING LOVE

The minister is committed to the exploration and transmission of truth. No less sacred, however, is his responsibility to people. The pastor is in constant tension between these priorities. He is under obligation to present a clear understanding of Christ's view of humanity. And what is that? Jesus gave the human race a new concept of itself! It is the liberation love brings, the steadfastness faith creates, the startling proclamation that every person, regardless of lineage or station, is a child of God.

No one should have a finer view of mankind, a more persuasive syllogism for loving and serving, than your pastor. Through observation, confrontation, teaching and by example, you gain from him a redemptive view of life. This is not easy. For instance, it is difficult for a minister to daily face and attempt to correct prejudice. It took me a long time to help a white friend move up the human scale in his conversation from "nigger" to "black" person. Eventually he came to the place where, when he would slip and use the humiliating word, he would apologize. Persistent love produces the miracle of change.

When Dr. Ernest Fremont Tittle, distinguished Methodist preacher of Evanston, Illinois, was honored by his congregation on the occasion of his twenty-fifth anniversary as its pastor, a businessman who was not at first enamored by the dynamic pastor was heard to say, "I remarked the other day, 'How Dr. Tittle has changed.' Then I caught myself and said, after thinking about it for a minute, 'No, *I* have changed!' "

THE LANGUAGE OF LOVE

Love can be a meaningless word. It is uniquely employed in today's rhetoric. Early evangelists and scholars used the word with delicate and precise meaning. The Greek world, with its definitive language, helps us comprehend the word *love. Philia* deals with love in general, such as love for oneself, for another, family, race, nation, or church. It is a satisfying but limited definition that scarcely transcends friendship.

Erōs expresses sexual desire and passionate aspiration. The word is not used in the New Testament. It embraces beauty and excellence, the charming and powerful. *Erōs* is the kind of love that frequently views another as a threat. It cultivates people for personal advancement. *Erōs* is possession.

Philia and erōs, helpful as they are in comprehending the dimensions of love, are incapable of communicating the love residing in God and Jesus Christ. So, the word *agapē* includes everything encompassed by *philia* and *erōs* and much, much more. It connotes love between God and man.

Unlike *philia* and *erōs, agapē* is suffused with freedom, justice, ethics, and universality. It focuses on people. It is neither self-serving nor defensive. *Agapē* seeks no rewards, keeps no score, expects no favors in return for services. It loves those of different cultures, races, and tastes. One loves because he was first loved by God! This contagious, covenantal, redemptive quality of love cements God's creation in purposeful unity and supportiveness. Such love is often painful. However difficult, *agapē* proclaims and confirms every person a child of God, possessing dignity, incalculable worth, and designed destiny.

Paul saw the uniqueness of Christian love as exceeding the gifts of knowledge, prophecy, philanthropy, mystery, power, and first-century virtues. The scholarly apostle reduced the essence of being to three ingredients: faith, hope, and love. "The greatest of these is love" (1 Cor. 13:13). God, being the author and dispenser of love, decided to release it through his Son, so Christian love is the result of God's primary decision to love his children; Jesus embodied it.

Love is the last survivor!

PROFILES OF LOVE

In *Les Miserables,* the French poet-novelist of the nineteenth century, Victor Hugo, introduces Jean Valjean, who was released from prison after serving nineteen years. The original sentence was five years for stealing a loaf of bread to feed his starving sister and her family. With each attempt to escape, Valjean's punishment was increased. While in prison he astonished observers by exhibitions of extraordinary physical strength; later he attracted individuals because of his exceptional courage and compassion.

The yellow passport he carried made it difficult for the ex-convict to find food, work, or lodging. Finally, he stumbled into the home of the Bishop of Digne, a saintly man who graciously provided him hospitality. During the night Jean Valjean stole the bishop's silverware. Quickly apprehended by the police, the thief and stolen articles were returned to the bishop. Without censure the forgiving churchman gave the desperate man what he had taken plus a pair of coveted candlesticks.

The bishop's attitude was incomprehensible but impressive. He asked the perplexed stranger to use the silver as a means of living an honest life. Subsequently Valjean's ministries of love multiplied.

Eventually, as Father Madeleine, operator of a small factory, mayor of the city, caring for Cosette, an illegitimate girl, risking his life for others, Jean Valjean endeared himself to all who knew him. When dying he bequeathed the candlesticks to Cosette, declaring he had tried to be worthy of the bishop's faith in him.

Every minister could wish his life might be as worthy of imitation as was that of Victor Hugo's Bishop of Digne. Your pastor's forgiving, redeeming spirit penetrates the parish and community in myriad ways. His love is constant and contagious. You are a recipient of it.

Both clergy and laity covet the staying power of Charles Lamb. This nineteenth century essayist and literary critic came home one day to discover that Mary, his mentally deranged sister, had murdered their parents. Refusing to commit her to an institution, he gave up his position to care for her. Depending entirely on his writing for their support, Charles Lamb looked after his sister for twenty-seven long years. When asked how he managed, he humbly replied, "I took the days one at a time."

What a lesson in love!

While I was visiting a friend in Bulawayo, Southern Rhodesia, our conversation naturally turned to the man from whom that early territory derived its name, Cecil John Rhodes. Born at Bishop's Stortford in Hertfordshire, England, in 1853, son of a clergyman, he went searching for a more compatible climate because of poor health. South Africa agreed with him. After several academic interruptions, Cecil Rhodes finally graduated from Oxford University. By now his financial resources were considerable.

This remarkable man's obsession with peace catapulted him into politics, projects of philanthropy, and eventually the establishment of the famous scholarships at Oxford that bear his name.

When I asked my companion why Mr. Rhodes, who made a fortune in diamonds, did not pursue the discovery of gold with similar zest, he answered, "The story goes that during the early leasing days of the better gold fields, a friend of Rhodes lay desperately ill. The popular and immensely wealthy Britisher denied himself the privilege of participating to sit by his friend's bed day and night until he died." Whether authentic or apocryphal, the report embodies the meaning of lasting love; it generates admiration and inspires one to praise the Lord of love.

A remarkable Christian of our time is Mother Teresa of Calcutta, India. Born of peasant stock in Yugoslavia, she eventually became a teacher, later a streetworker with Sisters of the Missionaries of Charity. This extraordinary soul leads a highly disciplined life, rising at 4:30 every morning for mass and meditation before beginning the long, arduous day.

This saint of the streets, epitome of *agapē*, says, "Welfare is for a purpose—an admirable and a necessary one—whereas Christian love is for a person." She is so sensitive to human need that the squeak of a discarded fetus, or the cry of an abandoned child, are echoes of the Babe of Bethlehem. Lepers, the homeless, and the hungry—all know her compassion. Mother Teresa refers to their Home for the Dying as a place where derelicts and the poorest of the poor may "die within sight of a living face."

Anyone who has observed the indescribable congestion, inhaled the aroma of cow dung and human excretion intensified by the heat of Calcutta's streets, can appreciate all the more the dedication of this saintly soul.

Love so amazing!

ECHOES OF LOVE

There is a well-known rural parish in Virginia that bears the name Perseverance. It is a phenomenal church where succeeding generations feed back into the life and witness of the congregation. One of its pastors, whose tenure exceeded two decades, was a carpenter. At the time of his homegoing, a colleague said of him, "Walter . . . is remembered in every chicken coop and house in the community." Whatever needed building or repairing, neighbors consulted the finest carpenter available, "the preacher!"

Many ministers have expertise in fields other than theology that increase rapport and enhance communication and appreciation. You may be surprised at what your pastor is doing for others. No model of ministry, however, will ever surpass or replace the genuineness of a pastor's love for the Lord and for his people.

Hearing a renowned pulpiteer one Sunday morning, another distinguished minister greeted him after worship, "You love to preach, don't you?"

"Yes, I do," came the immediate reply.

"Do you love those to whom you preach?"

This, of course, is a much deeper, more searching question. Irrespective of the nature of your pastor's call, size of parish, job description, compensation, it is love that motivates him to serve. Love sustains him. Some ministers are more flamboyant, self-serving, unlovable than others. But beneath the Sunday silhouette, robe and stole, suit and habit, is a person who strives to hear and leave echoes of love.

THE LIFE OF LOVE

Liv Ullmann says in *Changing,* "Love has many faces." And so it does. But no face ever mirrored the goodness of God like Jesus! In writing to the Corinthians, Paul declared that the glory of God was "in the face of Christ" (2 Cor. 4:6). Scholars suggest the word "face" here employed is not limited to countenance and physical features. The usage is called synecdoche, a figure of speech where one part is used for the whole.

We have no authentic likeness of Christ. Sculptors and artists have incited our imagination, but no one knows the precise profile of the Galilean.

In speaking of "the face of Christ," Paul is referring not only to his profile, but to his personality and character—his total being. The man of Nazareth was "good news" incarnate, the Word made flesh, undeniable truth, unquenchable light. Jesus was and is the Alpha and the Omega of Christian faith. "In him was life, and the life was the light of men" (John 1:4).

The Lord's face reflected gladness and joy, uncontaminated peace, beckoning salvation. To look upon this man sent of God was to encounter love; to hear him was to feel the warmth of love; to touch him was to be transformed by love.

Your pastor is not perfect. Because he is human, he sometimes loses his composure. His concern for his flock may cause him, at times, to be too aggressive. Being a disciple of truth, he is often involved in controversy. Overburdened with responsibilities, he may become delinquent in his own stewardship. Available to the community, he is often unavailable to his congregation and family. However, at the core of his being is love. To see him is to feel better; to talk with him is to be encouraged; to pray with him is to find the will to begin again.

THE PRESENCE OF LOVE

Our fluid, frightening world has greatly expanded and intensified vocabularies. New words have emerged, and older ones have been redefined. One is the word *presence*. Politically, we speak of a diplomatic representative as an American presence in a given country. This post exists for purposes of communication and conditioning for present negotiations as well as future transactions. A military presence suggests the recognition of a potential threat to people by a ruthless enemy. In America it also symbolizes our willingness to assist in case of an attack. The word *presence* is commonly used to connote availability and power. It says, "You're not alone."

The presence of your pastor in life's emergencies, tragedies, and celebrations symbolizes friendship. Deeper still, he is the visible, living, sustaining reminder of the availability of God. As Dr. Henri J. M. Nouwen of Yale Divinity School has written, the minister is forever making the connection "between the human story and the divine story." The faithful pastor is God's representative, agent of reconciliation, encouragement, and comfort.

Recapitulate some of the high and low moments in the Christian pilgrimage. There is the miracle of birth—not always successful. After ten years of married life, John and Joan, being told they could not bear children, adopted a little boy. Eighteen months later Joan delivered a still born baby. The pastor was in and out of the hospital every day. Later and for months he visited in the home, reassuring the despondent couple it was not God's will that the baby should die, nor should they censure themselves. No one can go through the traumatic losses of love without hearing the "footsteps" of souls involved. Later they articulated what they had frequently tried to say, "You were a tower of strength . . . we could not have made it without you."

There are not only moments of stress, but accelerating moments of growing gratitude: the baptismal service for a member of the family; the church wedding; the funeral of a loved one; accidents that change the composition of a family forever; promotions and demotions; honor and dishonor—all summon the pastor's presence. From the intertwining of such experiences a congregation and its minister become one in tenderness and strength, concern and commitment, trust and love.

Your church—like every congregation—is a crucible of love where the dross of human imperfections is tempered; the gifts and misgivings of pastor and people are fused into a redemptive fellowship; a mutual ministry of prayer and service wherein each sustains the other, the quality of their love attracting and enriching others.

Together you offer the "oil of gladness instead of mourning, the mantle of praise instead of a faint spirit" (Isa. 61:3a). Together you seek to actualize Isaiah's declaration: "You shall be called the priests of the Lord, men shall speak of you as the ministers of our God" (61:6).

In the pensive moments of your togetherness, you also hear the Lord asking, "Do you love me?" And, in unison, you answer, "Lord, you know we love you."

Knowing your pastor's love not only freshens memory of the Master, but also keeps alive Christ's charisma, his church and ministry in the world.